Volume 10
ECOLOGY

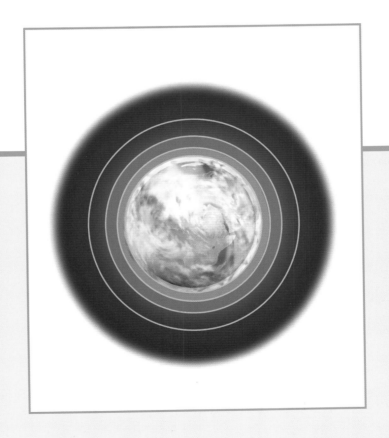

GROLIER

Published 2004 by Grolier
An imprint of Scholastic Library Publishing
Old Sherman Turnpike
Danbury, Connecticut 06816

FOR THE BROWN REFERENCE GROUP plc

Contributors:	John Woodward, Jen Green,
Consultant:	Mark Hostetler, Ph.D.
	Department of Wildlife
	Ecology & Conservation,
	IFAS, University of Florida
Consultant:	Val Kapos, Ph.D.
	University of Cambridge, UK
Project Editor:	Anne Wanjie
Deputy Editor:	Jim Martin
Development Editor:	Richard Beatty
Copy Editor:	Lesley Campbell-Wright
Designer:	Joan Curtis
Picture Researcher:	Becky Cox
Illustrators:	Darren Awuah, Richard Burgess,
	Mark Walker
Indexer:	Kay Ollerenshaw
Managing Editor:	Bridget Giles
Design Manager:	Lynne Ross
Production Director:	Alastair Gourlay
Editorial Director:	Lindsey Lowe

Printed and bound in Singapore

Volume ISBN 0-7172-5989-7
Set ISBN 0-7172-5979-X

Library of Congress Cataloging-in-Publication Data

Biology Matters!
   p. cm.
   Contents: v.1. Introduction to biology—v.2. Cell biology—v.3. Genetics—v.4.
Microorganisms—v.5. Plants—v.6. Animals—v.7. The human body—v.8.
Reproduction—v.9. Evolution—v.10. Ecology.
   ISBN 0-7172-5979-X (set : alk.paper)—ISBN 0-7172-5980-3 (v.1 : alk. paper)—
ISBN 0-7172-5981-1 (v.2 : alk. paper)—ISBN 0-7172-5982-X (v.3 : alk. paper)—
ISBN 0-7172-5983-8 (v.4 : alk. paper)—ISBN 0-7172-5984-6 (v.5 : alk. paper)—
ISBN 0-7172-5985-4 (v.6 : alk. paper)—ISBN 0-7172-5986-2 (v.7 : alk. paper)—
ISBN 0-7172-5987-0 (v.8 : alk. paper)—ISBN 0-7172-5988-9 (v.9 : alk. paper)—
ISBN 0-7172-5989-7 (v.10 : alk. paper)
   1. Biology—Juvenile literature. [1. Biology.] I. Grolier Publishing Company

QH309.2.B56 2004
507—dc22

                                        2003056942

ABOUT THIS SET

What could be more fascinating than the story of life? It is all told in *Biology Matters!* Across ten topical volumes this set reviews all fundamental life-science concepts. Each volume carefully introduces its topic, briefly examines the history, and fully displays all aspects of modern thinking about biology, ecology, evolution, genetics, cell biology, microbiology, life forms from every kingdom, and the human body. The clear text explains complex concepts and terms in full. Hundreds of photographs, artworks, and "Closeup" boxes provide details on key aspects. Simple, safe experiments encourage readers to explore biology in "Try This" boxes. "What Do You Think?" panels pose questions that test the reader's comprehension. "Applications" boxes show how biological knowledge enhances daily life and technology, while "Red Herring" boxes outline failed theories. "Hot Debate" panels illuminate the disagreements and discussions that rage in the biological sciences, and "Genetic Perspective" boxes outline the latest genetic research.

CONTENTS

Volume 10
Ecology

1 What Is Ecology?

Ecology is about the pattern of nature—it is the study of the interactions among living organisms and their environment.

Every living thing depends on other things for its survival. House sparrows living in a park have to find seeds to eat. The seeds come from plants that must find places to grow. Sparrows feed on insects too, and the insects need plants to eat. Sparrows also need air to breathe, water to drink, and places to lay eggs. So each sparrow is at the center of a web of relationships involving other living things and its surroundings, or environment. Ecology is the science that studies these types of relationships. Instead of concentrating only on a sparrow, ecologists study how it interacts with other organisms and its environment.

Food chains and webs
One of the most basic ideas in ecology is the food chain.

◀ *A gypsy moth caterpillar. Many caterpillars eat leaves, and many birds then eat the caterpillars. This link between leaf, caterpillar, and bird forms a food chain.*

Green plants make food from water, sunlight, and carbon dioxide (in the air) by a process called photosynthesis (see **5: 6–13**). Animals cannot do this, so they must eat other living organisms to get their food.

Caterpillars eat leaves and turn them into caterpillar flesh. In a simple food chain other animals, such as small birds, eat the caterpillars, and the birds themselves may be eaten by cats. However, the caterpillars are also eaten by other insects. Thus most food chains are not so simple. Several linked chains make up a food web.

Habitats and niches

All animals, plants, and other living organisms struggle to survive. Many organisms die, and only the best adapted live long enough to reproduce.

FOOD WEBS

This diagram shows a food web based on the plants and trees in a small forest. A food web is much more complicated than a simple food chain, in which each plant or animal provides food for just one other animal. The plants provide food for many insects, worms, and other small animals, which in turn provide food for larger animals, such as cats, moles, and many different types of birds.

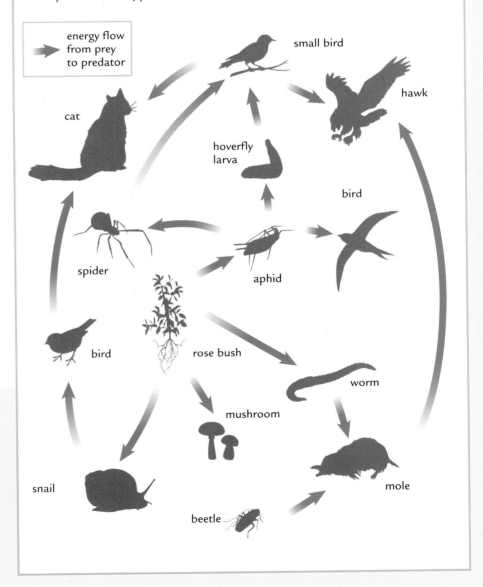

energy flow from prey to predator

small bird

hawk

cat

hoverfly larva

bird

spider

aphid

bird

rose bush

worm

mushroom

snail

mole

beetle

FIGURE OUT A FOOD WEB

Make a list of all the animals that live in your backyard or in a local park. Remember to include insects and other minibeasts, and all the animals with fur, feathers, or scales. Check out the animals in a book to see what they eat. Then try to arrange them in a food web like the one shown on page 5. It might get complicated!

ECOLOGICAL SURVEYS

By figuring out the relationships between plants and animals and their environment, an ecologist can try to predict what will happen if one part of the pattern is taken away. So if there is a plan to drain a mosquito-infested swamp, an ecologist can find out what other animals live in the swamp and how they might be affected. It may turn out that draining the swamp could destroy some rare and beautiful waterbirds.

Alligators in a swamp in Georgia could be affected if other animals or plants were removed from their habitat.

This process is called natural selection, the basis of evolution (see **9**: 4–7). What does "fittest" mean? That depends on the environment. A goldfish can survive very well in a pond, but it would die in a desert. A lizard can live in a desert, but it would freeze in the Arctic. Even if an animal or plant survives, it may not do as well as its neighbors. So over time it is crowded out. Every living organism has characteristics, or adaptations, that make them suited to their environment (see **5**: 14–23; **6**: 28–37). The place in which an animal or plant lives is called its habitat.

A habitat could be a rocky seashore or a tropical forest. Such places offer all kinds of ways in which animals and plants can live. Every species of living organism has its own special way of surviving in its habitat, and that is called its niche. For example, some birds specialize in eating large

POPULATIONS AND COMMUNITIES

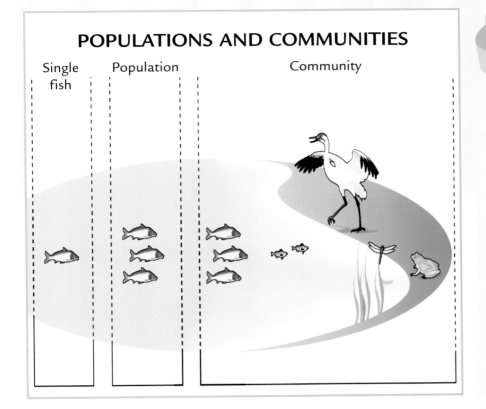

Single fish | Population | Community

ECOSYSTEM IN A JAR

Create your own mini ecosystem in a big glass jar by collecting some water from a pond in summer. Tell an adult before you go, and take care not to fall in! Fill your jar about three-quarters full. Then add some mud taken from the bottom of the pond. A layer one to two fingers thick should be enough. Add some water plants to produce oxygen. You can get them from the pond or at pet stores. Put your jar in a cool window, and wait for a while. The water will clear, and you may be surprised at what you can see. The plants and animals will keep each other healthy for a period of time.

fruits, while others feed on small insects. The two types of birds occupy different niches.

Population to community
A niche can be occupied by just one species. A small lake may have only enough food for one big predatory fish, such as a pike, but a large lake contains enough food for several pike, and they form a population. All the animals in a population are of the same species and occupy the same ecological niche. They share their lives with other populations of different animals and plants, and together these interacting populations form a community. So the fish, insects, birds, and plants in a lake make up a community.

Ecosystems
An ecological community can contain plants, animals, fungi, and microorganisms, such as bacteria. These living organisms share an environment that has nonliving elements, such as the climate (the typical weather experienced over a year), the soil, and the location, which might be an exposed, rocky headland or a sheltered, sandy beach. A river might be slow and muddy or swift and sparkling. The possibilities are endless.

MICROHABITATS AND COMMUNITIES

Most habitats are made of smaller microhabitats, such as the forest floor, a hole in a tree, or different layers of a tree. A forest usually has many different types of trees, and each tree can support its own community of animals. Different communities also live at different levels of the forest. One community lives on the forest floor, another in the understory, and yet another among the branches of the forest (top canopy, or branchy layer). Tropical forests have two or three canopy layers. More layers produce more communities. More communities creates greater biodiversity (range of life forms).

AMAZON RAINFOREST TREE

CANOPY
Birds and climbing animals live here.

UNDERSTORY
Butterflies, snakes, and some types of anteaters are among the animals that live in the forest understory.

FOREST FLOOR
Jaguars, warthogs, and many other animals inhabit the ground level.

Communities of living organisms interact with their nonliving environment in all kinds of ways. These interactions often control the types of living things present in the community. For example, most riverside plants cannot grow in an estuary (where the tide mixes with fresh water) because the water is too salty. Only salt-tolerant plants can grow in estuary shallows. Along with the animals that live among them these plants form a salt-marsh community. The cycle of complex interactions between the community and its environment is called an ecosystem.

Biomes
Any community in its environment can be called an ecosystem if it looks after itself. A small pond is an ecosystem because all the animals and plants in it get almost everything they need without leaving the water. The

plants make the oxygen and food that the animals need, and in turn the animals make the nutrients and carbon dioxide that the plants need. A forest could also be seen as an ecosystem. In some parts of the world forests cover vast areas. So do grasslands,

oceans, and deserts. A large geographical region that has its own distinctive climate, plants, and animals is called a biome and is generally made of several types of ecosystems. All the deserts on Earth form one biome; all the tropical forests make another (see 31).

▲ *The San Francisco Bay National Wildlife Refuge has a high biodiversity because it contains many different types of plant and animal species. These species include harbor seals, salt-marsh harvest mice, peregrine falcons, and pelicans.*

BIODIVERSITY

APPLICATIONS

Some ecological communities contain very few different species, usually because the habitat is very difficult to live in. Arctic communities contain a much smaller range of species than

rainforest communities. They have reduced biodiversity (variety of life; see **1**: 14–27). However, biodiversity can also change over time. If a wild prairie is turned into a giant wheatfield, its biodiversity

goes down. Nearly all the wild plants disappear, and most of the animals that used to eat them vanish too. Ecologists use biodiversity as a way of measuring how habitats are affected by land use.

2 Cycles of Nature

▲ *Plant-eating animals, such as this hare, gain their energy from plants, which, in turn, get their energy from the sun through photosynthesis.*

The living world is powered by the energy of the sun and uses basic raw materials that are constantly being recycled by natural processes.

All living organisms need energy to grow and reproduce. Nearly all of this energy comes from the sun. The energy is absorbed by plants, which use some of it to make energy-storing foods, such as starch, in a process called photosynthesis (see **5**: 6–13).

Herbivorous (plant-eating) animals, such as rabbits, eat plants and use the stored energy to power their own

APPLICATIONS

INDICATOR SPECIES

A creature such as a bald eagle (right) is at the topmost energy level of its ecosystem. A single eagle pair needs a lot of prey animals to support it. The prey, in turn, need to eat a huge number of plants.

If anything interrupts the food supply lower down the ecosystem, the eagles are the first to run out of food and leave. So eagles and similar big predators are indicator species; that is, they show if the ecosystem is healthy.

TROPHIC LEVELS

Foxes and hawks both eat rabbits, but usually they do not eat each other. Ecologists say foxes and hawks are in the same trophic level in an ecosystem. Rabbits and mice eat grass and clover, which are on the trophic level below them. As a result of energy losses, the biomass of each ecosystem level is about one-tenth that of the level below. So, 2,200 pounds (1,000kg) of grass and clover support 220 pounds (100kg) of rabbits and mice but only 22 pounds (10kg) of foxes and hawks. Thus there are many more rabbits than foxes in an ecosystem.

activities. They also store some of the energy in their own bodies. If the rabbits are eaten by carnivores (meat eaters), such as foxes, the stored energy is passed on again.

Producers and consumers

Plants that produce food using the sun's energy are producers. Animals, which get their energy by eating, are consumers. All consumers rely on the producers lower down the food chain. In a meadow these producers might be grass plants. There are usually many levels of consumers—the grass may be eaten by rabbits, which are then eaten by foxes, which, in turn, may be eaten by eagles.

At each level a lot of the energy is used up or lost. The total weight (or biomass; the total amount of living

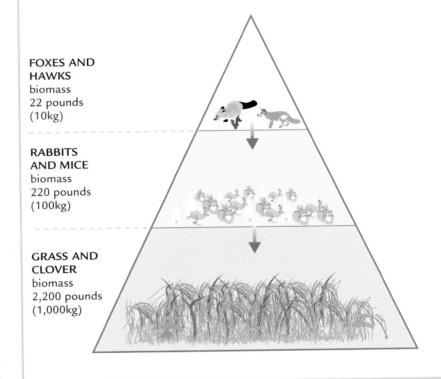

FOXES AND HAWKS
biomass
22 pounds
(10kg)

RABBITS AND MICE
biomass
220 pounds
(100kg)

GRASS AND CLOVER
biomass
2,200 pounds
(1,000kg)

TRY THIS

ECOLOGICAL PYRAMID

Look at the food web on page 5. Which animals are not eaten by others and are at the top trophic level? Look up their weight in a book. Assume there are two of each, and add up their weights to get their biomass. Then arrange all the other animals in trophic levels, and figure out their biomass, remembering that each level weighs about 10 times the one above it. The weight at the bottom of the pyramid should be a lot more than at the top!

HIGH-FIBER DIET

If you gather a snail from your backyard and put it in a tank with an empty jelly jar, it can eat the jar's paper label. The paper is made of cellulose, or plant fiber, and snails are among the few animals that can digest cellulose without help and turn it into sugar.

Other animals, such as cows, have millions of bacteria in their stomachs that do the same job. In the process they produce a lot of a carbon-containing gas called methane, which passes back into the air to rejoin the carbon cycle.

CARBON CONVERSION

Water plants gather carbon from carbon dioxide dissolved in water. If you put a pondweed such as *Elodea* in a glass jar of water and put the jar in bright sunlight, you will see small bubbles forming on the leaves. The bubbles are pure oxygen, which is released as the plant changes carbon dioxide and water into sugar.

material) of grass eaten by the rabbits is not all turned into rabbit flesh. Much of it is used up by hopping around and other activities, and only a small amount is stored. In addition, animal digestion is imperfect and cannot capture all of the energy of a food item. The same happens at every level of consumption. So it takes a lot of grass to support a colony of rabbits and a lot of rabbits to support a family of foxes.

The carbon cycle

The sun is a virtually limitless source of energy. However, the raw materials of life are not limitless and are

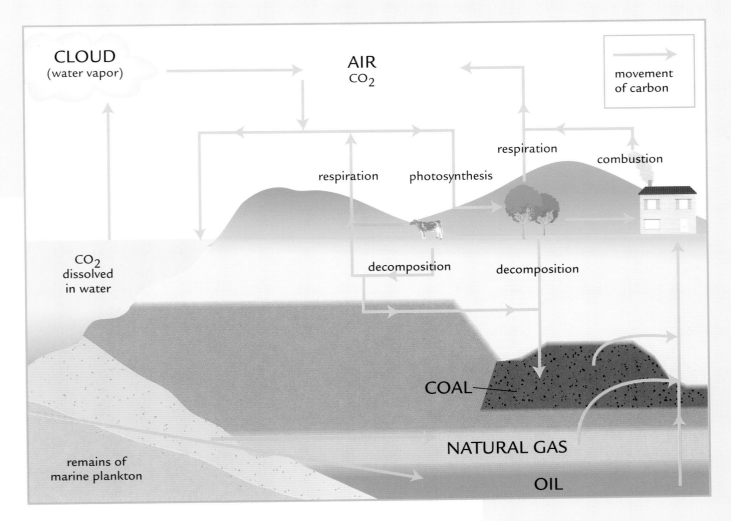

CLOUD
(water vapor)

AIR
CO_2

movement
of carbon

respiration   photosynthesis

respiration

combustion

CO_2
dissolved
in water

decomposition

decomposition

COAL

NATURAL GAS

remains of
marine plankton

OIL

constantly recycled. One of the most important is carbon (see **1**: 28–37), the element that is the main ingredient of oil, soot, and diamonds. Carbon has a special ability to combine with other elements to make molecules of different substances, including plant and animal tissues.

Plants get carbon from carbon dioxide gas in the air. They also take in water, which is made of hydrogen and oxygen. They use the sun's energy to combine carbon, hydrogen, and oxygen into compounds called carbohydrates, substances such as sugar and starch, which store the sun's energy. Plants use sugars to fuel cell activities or store starch. They also use sugar to make a tough plant fiber called cellulose, the main part of plant tissue.

Releasing carbon
Plant-eating animals digest the sugar and starch in plants

▲ *The carbon cycle shows how carbon moves around Earth. Plants take carbon dioxide from the atmosphere in photosynthesis and return it during the processes of respiration (see **1**: 35) and decomposition. Over many years some carbon is kept away from the cycle by dead organisms that form deposits of rocks and fossil fuels. Later it goes back into the cycle during weathering of the rocks or burning of the fossil fuels.*

HOT DEBATE

FOSSIL FUELS

When plants and animals die, the carbon in their bodies is usually recycled by other organisms and returned to the atmosphere (air around Earth). This recycling happens as the tissues decay or are broken down by microorganisms, such as bacteria. If these microorganisms cannot act on the tissues, after compression the remains become fossilized as carbon-rich coal or oil. The energy locked up in these tissues is also fossilized. If these fossil fuels are burned, the chemical reaction releases both the stored energy and the carbon, which returns to the air as carbon dioxide.

The huge quantities of fossil fuels burned over the last 150 years have released carbon that has been stored for millions of years. This activity has increased the amount of carbon dioxide in the atmosphere. Carbon dioxide is a greenhouse gas (see 59). It is the main cause of global warming (the increase in Earth's average air temperature), which has sparked debate worldwide (see 25).

▼ *The way nitrogen moves around Earth is called the nitrogen cycle. Plants and animals use nitrogen after it is chemically changed into nitrates by bacteria. Nitrogen returns to the soil when animals and plants die and by the addition of manure to soil. Denitrifying bacteria release nitrogen into the air again.*

and change them into a sugar called glucose. They use it to build their own tissues and as an energy-rich fuel. By combining the sugar with oxygen, which they get by breathing, plants change it back into carbon dioxide and water. This chemical reaction, called respiration, releases all the energy that the plants soaked up from the sun. The animals breathe out the carbon dioxide into the atmosphere, where it is available to the plants again (see **5**: 6–13).

The nitrogen cycle
Carbon is a vital part of living tissue because it can combine

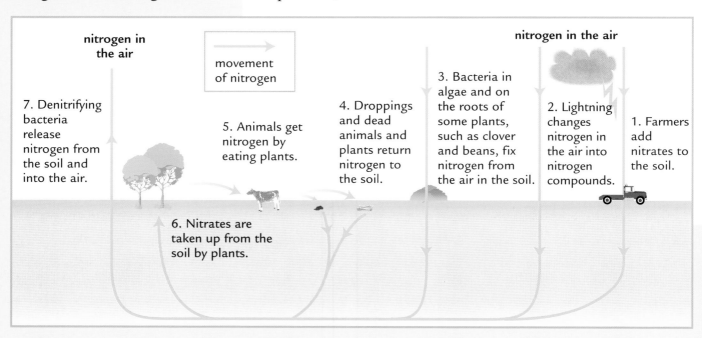

nitrogen in the air

movement of nitrogen

nitrogen in the air

7. Denitrifying bacteria release nitrogen from the soil and into the air.

5. Animals get nitrogen by eating plants.

4. Droppings and dead animals and plants return nitrogen to the soil.

3. Bacteria in algae and on the roots of some plants, such as clover and beans, fix nitrogen from the air in the soil.

2. Lightning changes nitrogen in the air into nitrogen compounds.

1. Farmers add nitrates to the soil.

6. Nitrates are taken up from the soil by plants.

with other elements to make complex molecules. One of the most important of these elements is nitrogen, which links with carbon, hydrogen, and oxygen to form proteins (see **1**: 28–37). Proteins are the main building blocks of animal tissue, and they are also very important to plants.

Nitrogen gas makes up 78 percent of the air, but it does not combine easily with other substances. That makes nitrogen almost useless to plants and animals in its raw state. However, in a process called nitrogen fixation some microorganisms turn nitrogen into compounds that are used by plants and can be turned into plant tissue. These microorganisms include bacteria that live in the soil and on the roots of plants such as clover and beans.

Decay and recycling

Plants use nitrogen to build proteins. When animals eat plants or each other, they digest the proteins and use their ingredients to make new proteins. When plants and animals die, bacteria and other microorganisms attack the proteins and break them down, releasing nitrogen compounds into the soil. The plants can absorb these types

MANURE AND FERTILIZER

Animal dung is made up of half-digested food remains mixed with a lot of digestive juices and bacteria. Once on the ground, it decays quickly, releasing a lot of nitrogen compounds that can be taken up by plants. This action is part of the natural nitrogen cycle. Farmers can take advantage of it by spreading farmyard manure on their fields (below). As the manure breaks down, it adds nitrogen compounds and other nutrients, such as phosphorus and potassium, to the soil. They make the soil more fertile (rich in nutrients), so farm crops grow better. Farmers can also use fertilizer made in a factory, which contains nitrogen, phosphorus, and potassium. The chemical abbreviations for these elements are N, P, and K, so it is often called NPK fertilizer.

ROOT NODULES

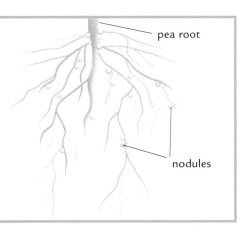

pea root

nodules

Try growing some pea plants in pots. They sprout easily because each seed contains a lot of stored energy and protein. Eventually, however, they have to absorb extra nutrients through their roots. If you dig up a pea plant when it is tall, you will find tiny nodules (bumps) on its roots. They contain the bacteria that gather nitrogen from air in the soil and turn it into a form the plant can use.

HOT DEBATE

NITRATE POLLUTION

The factory-made fertilizers used by farmers contain nitrogen in a form called nitrate, which is ideal for use by plants. That makes it instantly effective, unlike farmyard manure, which has to be broken down to nitrate by soil bacteria. However, nitrate dissolves in water, which is how the plants absorb it. During wet weather the nitrates wash off the fields and into ponds and rivers. They then fertilize the water, causing massive growth of microscopic plantlike algae (see **4**: 27). This upsets the aquatic ecosystem, and so there is a lot of debate about the use of nitrate fertilizers.

of compounds into their roots with water and recycle them to make more plant proteins.

The phosphorus cycle
Carbon and nitrogen exist in gases in the atmosphere, but other raw materials of life, such as phosphorus, potassium, calcium, and sodium, are normally solid minerals or dissolved in water.

Phosphorus is essential to living things. It is a vital ingredient of nucleic acids, such as DNA (see **3**: 26–37). Plants need phosphorus for healthy root growth, while animals use phosphorus and

APPLICATIONS

GUANO

Fish are the main food for millions of ocean birds, which breed on coasts and islands. These breeding sites become smothered in bird

calcium to form teeth and bones. Both minerals occur in rocks. When rocks are weathered into mineral grains, they become part of the soil. Plants take them up in soil water and build them into their tissues. That makes phosphorus and

Guano-covered rocks on a coast, Baja California, Mexico.

CLOSEUP

EXTRA MINERALS

Animals need some mineral nutrients that plants do not. These minerals include sodium, an ingredient in table salt. Since most plants do not need sodium, they do not absorb it. Thus, plant-eating animals may not get any sodium in their diet. They often deal with the problem by licking the mineral from rocks or soil that contain sodium.

In Peru macaws (above) and other birds visit clay-licks to get mineral supplements. The minerals may also neutralize the effects of toxic fruits and seeds the birds eat.

calcium available to plant-eating animals and, in turn, to meat-eating animals. When plants and animals die, their tissues decay, and so the phosphorus and other nutrients pass back into the soil.

Recycled rock

As rainwater drains through soil and into small streams, it carries with it nutrients, such as phosphorus, calcium, and other minerals. The streams drain into rivers that flow to the sea. Thus these minerals become available to aquatic animals, such as fish. When the fish die, their remains drift to the ocean floor, where the minerals gradually build up in layers that turn into solid rock. After millions of years the rock may be pushed to the surface and eventually form more soil.

dung (guano). Guano is rich in phosphorus because of all the fish bones swallowed by the birds. On some sites the guano has built up over thousands of years to form thick layers. In the 19th century these guano deposits were mined to make phosphorus-rich fertilizer for farm crops.

WHAT DO YOU THINK?

AROUND AND AROUND

Simple nutrients like carbon, nitrogen, and phosphorus are constantly cycling around the global ecosystem. Some, such as nitrogen, cycle quickly. Others, such as the carbon in fossil fuels, cycle over millions of years. Since everything cycles around eventually, does it matter how these substances are used? Does it matter, for example, if people burn a lot of coal and oil and release a lot of carbon dioxide into the atmosphere?

3 Climate and Earth

▲ Palm trees bend under the force of powerful winds called hurricanes, which blow at more than 75 miles per hour (120km/h). Hurricanes start above ocean areas in the tropics.

Each place on Earth has its own climate, which is that region's regular pattern of weather. Any factors that affect a region's climate will have an effect on the types of living organisms that thrive there.

Climate is a broad picture of the average weather conditions experienced in a region over many years. The sun provides the energy that drives the weather and so produces climate. It causes winds to blow and moisture to circulate between the atmosphere and the surface of Earth in a continual process called the water cycle (see 26). All the day-to-day weather conditions, such as sunshine, showers, storms,

THE SUN'S POWER

The sun's rays travel in parallel lines toward Earth. They strike down from directly above at the equator, where they are concentrated on a relatively small area. So the climate in the tropics is always hot. The sun beats down less directly in temperate regions, which are north and south of the tropics,

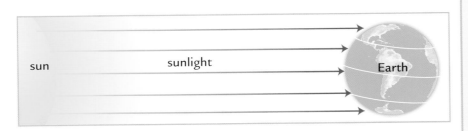

so they have a cooler climate. At the polar regions, where Earth's surface is most curved, the rays strike at a sharp (oblique) angle and are spread out over a much wider area. The rays also have farther to travel through the atmosphere, which absorbs heat, so the polar climate is cold.

and blizzards, are caused by the sun heating various parts of Earth by different amounts. Differences in temperature produce variations in air pressure, the force exerted on Earth's surface by the weight of the air around it. Changes in air pressure then cause air masses to move from one place to another, which produces winds. Winds may bring warm or cool temperatures and dry or rainy spells.

Factors affecting climate

The three main factors influencing climate are latitude (distance from the equator), altitude (height above sea level), and how far a region is from the sea. Latitude is a very important factor. Earth's curving surface enables various regions to receive differing amounts of the sun's heat.

INTO THE PAST

CLIMATE ZONES

Austrian scientist Wladimir Köppen (1846–1940) was among the first to classify regions according to climate. Köppen studied how plant life in different parts of the world is affected by climate. In 1918 he produced a classification listing five main climate zones: tropical/rainy; dry; temperate/rainy; cold/snowy; and polar. Köppen's classification is still used, but many modern climatologists (climate experts) distinguish at least a dozen climate zones, as shown on the map below.

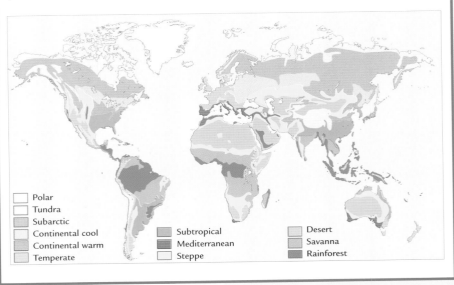

Polar
Tundra
Subarctic
Continental cool
Continental warm
Temperate
Subtropical
Mediterranean
Steppe
Desert
Savanna
Rainforest

EARTH'S SEASONS

The tilting of Earth on its axis as it goes around the sun means that the northern hemisphere is tipped closer to the sun in June, making longer and warmer days in the season called summer. In June the southern hemisphere is tipped farther from the sun, causing winter, a season with colder and shorter days. The opposite happens in December.

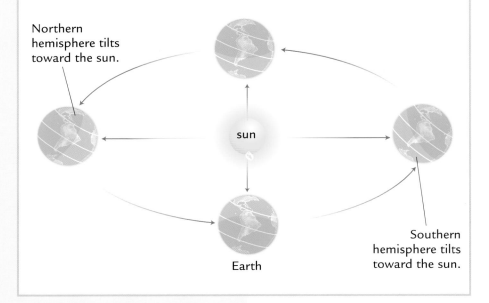

Northern hemisphere tilts toward the sun.

sun

Earth

Southern hemisphere tilts toward the sun.

The seasons

Many parts of the world experience regular seasonal changes because Earth tilts on its axis (an imaginary line linking the North and South poles) at an angle of 23.5° as it orbits the sun. At any time one hemisphere (half of Earth) leans toward the sun and has summer with long hours of daylight. The other hemisphere tilts away and has winter with short days.

Seasonal changes are least noticeable in the tropics, the regions closest to the equator that always face the sun. However, some parts of the tropics have a dry and a rainy season. Many temperate regions have four seasons: spring, summer, fall, and winter. The poles have the greatest variation in temperature and day length. For part of the summer each pole is

TRY THIS RECORDING SEASONAL CHANGES

Monitor how seasonal changes affect the area where you live by keeping records. Record temperatures at regular times each day for one week each month, and note the hours of daylight. You could also record how the seasons affect local plants and animal behavior. For example, local mammals and reptiles may not be seen in winter because they hibernate, and some local birds may migrate.

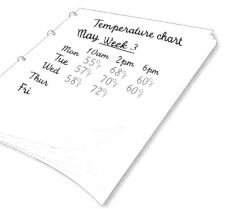

Temperature chart
May Week 3

	10am	2pm	6pm
Mon	55°	68°	60°
Tue	57°	70°	60°
Wed	58°	72°	
Thur			
Fri			

CLIMATE ZONES ON MOUNTAINS

Altitude affects the types of plants that grow at different heights on mountains. Generally, higher up on mountains only small plants grow. For example, broad-leaved trees such as oaks may grow at a mountain's base, but only cold-resistant bathed in weak sunlight for 24 hours a day. For part of the winter the sun never rises. Arctic plants cope with this by becoming dormant (inactive) in winter. Many animals hibernate (enter a sleeplike state) or migrate (move away) to avoid the cold.

Altitude

Height above sea level, or altitude, also affects a region's climate because the thinner air at higher altitudes absorbs less of the sun's heat. The temperature drops about 1 °C for every 500 feet (150m) climbed. Mountain climates are thus much cooler than the surrounding lowlands, with shorter summers and longer winters. The tops of high mountains near the equator, such as Kilimanjaro in East Africa, are always covered with snow.

Maritime and continental climates

Distance from the sea also affects a region's climate. The oceans absorb the sun's heat more slowly than the land but retain their warmth longer. Coasts may also be warmed or cooled by ocean currents and are thus usually milder than

▲ Kilimanjaro, the tallest mountain in Africa, is 19,340 feet (5,895m) at its highest point. Although it is just a few miles from the equator, it is always capped by snow because the thinner air at high altitude absorbs less of the sun's heat.

conifers, such as pine trees, thrive higher up. Even higher, beyond a zone called the tree line, there are no trees, only low-growing plants. The kinds of plants that can grow at that altitude are usually found in alpine tundra regions. Beyond the snow line no vegetation grows because the climate there is too harsh.

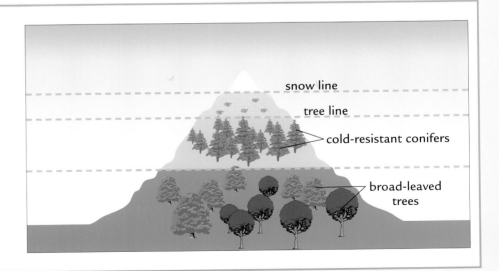

snow line

tree line

cold-resistant conifers

broad-leaved trees

regions far inland and also wetter because winds blowing inshore off the sea are laden with moisture. Coastal regions have a maritime climate, while areas far inland have a continental climate.

The atmosphere

The atmosphere is a blanket of gases surrounding Earth like the peel on an orange. It extends about 450 miles (720km) into space. The main gases in the atmosphere are nitrogen (78 percent) and oxygen (21 percent). Smaller amounts of carbon dioxide, water vapor, nitrous oxide, ozone, and other gases are also present. They are important

▲ *The cloud formation on the coastline of a beach in Kauai, Hawaii, is typical of a maritime climate.*

LAYERS IN THE ATMOSPHERE

About 75 percent of all the air in the atmosphere exists below 6½ miles (10.5km). The air becomes progressively thinner closer to space. Scientists distinguish five main layers in the atmosphere. The lowest layer, the troposphere, extends to 12 miles (19km) above the planet's surface. Most weather occurs here. Above that is a calm layer, the stratosphere, extending to about 30 miles (48km) up. Aircraft fly here to avoid turbulence. Most meteors burn up in the layer beyond, the mesophere, 30 to 50 miles (48–80km) up. The thermosphere (50 to 280 miles, 80–450km, up) is a layer containing electrically charged particles. Beyond that a layer of very thin air called the exosphere extends into space.

Jet planes fly in the stratosphere. The ozone layer is in the upper part of this layer.

The troposphere contains three-quarters of the water vapor in the atmosphere. Nearly all the clouds, rain, and snow occur in this layer.

The mesosphere has the same mixture of oxygen, nitrogen, and carbon dioxide as lower layers, but it has very little water vapor.

Spectacular light effects called auroras can be seen in the thermosphere.

because they trap the sun's warmth. The atmosphere shields Earth from harmful radiation, keeps out the cold of space, and contains oxygen for living things to breathe. Without it life on Earth would be impossible.

The ozone layer

A layer of ozone gas is present in the stratosphere about 15 miles (24km) above Earth's surface. Ozone, a form of oxygen, is a bluish gas. The ozone layer shields Earth from harmful ultraviolet (UV) radiation in sunlight. UV rays can cause illnesses such as cancer and eye damage in animals and also harm plants, including phytoplankton, a major food source in the sea.

The greenhouse effect

Carbon dioxide, methane, water vapor, and other gases in the atmosphere act as a barrier that traps heat rising from Earth's surface

CLOSEUP

OZONE LOSS

In the 1980s scientists discovered that a hole in the atmosphere containing less ozone than normal was appearing over Antarctica each spring. During the 1990s ozone holes over Antarctica and the Arctic got steadily bigger. Scientists showed that chorofluorocarbons (CFCs) were mainly causing the damage. CFCs are chemicals used in the manufacture of refrigerators, polystyrene packaging, and aerosol spray cans, and in air conditioning. The loss of ozone has caused an increase in skin cancer in people and animals in recent years (see 59).

Old refrigerators containing CFCs threaten the ozone layer.

CHANGING SEA LEVELS

The diagrams below show (**a**) the position of Florida's coastline 18,000 years ago, when the sea level was lower than present, and (**b**) and (**c**) the possible situation if global warming causes the polar ice cap to melt. Most of Florida would disappear completely.

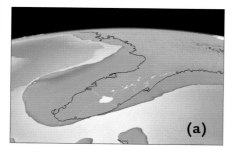
(a)

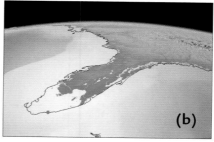
(b)

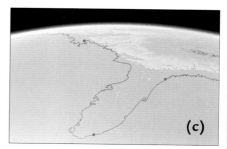
(c)

Sea level 18,000 years ago, 394 feet (120m) lower than present.

Possible future sea level 17 feet (5m) higher than present.

Possible future sea level 170 feet (50m) higher than present.

APPLICATIONS

A COLD SPELL

Between about 1400 and 1800 Earth had a mini-ice age, when winters were much colder than they are now. Rivers and lakes froze over regularly, and frost fairs were held on the ice. During the last frost fair on the Thames River in London in 1814 (below) the thick ice supported the weight of an elephant. Landscapes by European artists showing frozen waterways in winter were once a common sight.

and prevents it from escaping into space. These gases have a similar effect as the glass in a greenhouse, so this process is called the greenhouse effect. For millions of years the greenhouse effect has created a warm environment on Earth that has allowed living organisms to flourish here. Scientists now fear that human-made pollution is increasing Earth's greenhouse effect and causing temperatures to rise above normal, an effect called global warming. A result might then be melting of the polar ice, causing the oceans to flood coastal land.

GLOBAL WARMING

In the last 200 years Earth's climate has been growing steadily warmer in a process called global warming. Temperatures rose by 1°F (0.5 °C) in the last 50 years and may now be rising more rapidly. Scientists have found that human-made pollution is causing the warming. As people burn fossil fuels in cars, power plants, homes, and factories, more carbon dioxide is added to the atmosphere, increasing global warming.

Climate change

Earth's climate appears to stay the same, but it changes very slowly. Long, cold periods called ice ages gradually give way to warmer ones. Scientists believe these long-term changes are caused because Earth wobbles slightly as it orbits the sun. During the past 2 million years a total of 15 ice ages have come and gone. The last major ice age ended about 10,000 years ago. During these cold periods ice covered large parts of what are now temperate regions, including much of North America and Europe.

Scientists find out about Earth's climate in the past using various techniques. In one method samples of ice buried deep in the polar regions are collected. Examination of these ice cores reveals what the climate was

TREE RINGS

Studying tree rings provides information about climate. Trees produce these trunk rings as they add new layers of wood beneath the bark each year during the growing season.

Find a tree that has been cut down, and study the tree rings to find out about climate during the tree's lifetime. The newest rings are on the outside, with the oldest growth near the center. Find the wide, light rings, which represent the spring and summer seasons, when the tree grew quickest. A smaller dark ring, representing winter growth, separates these wider rings. Count in from the bark to find out when these rings occurred (one year for each light ring). You can also count all the rings to find out the tree's age when it was cut down. Some bristlecone pines in the western United States are 4,000 years old.

THE WATER CYCLE

Moisture moves constantly between the air, land, and oceans in a process called the water cycle. The sun's heat causes moisture from oceans, lakes, and wet ground to evaporate (turn into water vapor). At cooler temperatures the moisture condenses (turns into liquid) to form clouds, which later shed rain or snow. When rain falls, the excess moisture not absorbed by the soil or taken up by plants drains into streams, rivers, and lakes, which eventually empty into the ocean, and so the cycle goes around again.

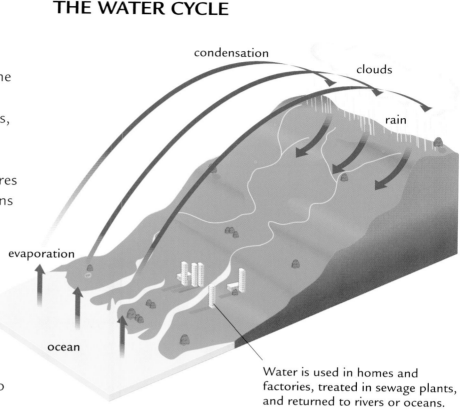

condensation

clouds

rain

evaporation

ocean

Water is used in homes and factories, treated in sewage plants, and returned to rivers or oceans.

like many thousands of years ago, when snow fell to form the ice. Studying tree rings also yields information about climate (see 25).

Life-giving water

As well as oxygen from the atmosphere, all organisms need water, which makes up on average 75 percent of living things. Water exists on Earth in three forms—as a liquid, as a gas (water vapor), and in solid form as ice. Moisture collects in the atmosphere to form clouds made up of millions of tiny

RED HERRING

EARLY IDEAS ABOUT EROSION

Before 1800 most people believed that Earth was only a few thousand years old. A group of scientists called the Neptunists thought that all landforms had been shaped by a series of disasters in the distant past and had not changed since then. Scotsman Dr. James Hutton (1726–1797) was among the first to say that Earth was much older—millions rather than thousands of years old. Hutton rightly believed that natural forces such as waves, wind, and water were continually shaping Earth.

water droplets. Clouds shed moisture as precipitation in the form of rain, hail, or snow.

Soil and climate

Soil forms the link between the living world and the non-living rocks that make up Earth. Most living things on land need the soil either directly or indirectly to live. Plants root in the soil and take water and nourishment from it. An area of soil just 1 foot (30cm) square may contain literally millions of organisms, including insects, spiders, slugs, and worms, and microscopic bacteria and fungi. Many of them help break down plant and animal remains so their nutrients return to fertilize the soil.

Over thousands of years soil is slowly created by the forces of weather, as ice, frost, wind, and running water break down the rocks at Earth's surface in a process called erosion. Different types of soil, including chalk, clay, sand, and peat, are present in different regions. The type of soil depends on many factors, including climate, vegetation, and the composition of the underlying rock.

TRY THIS

SAVING WATER

The world's rainfall is not evenly distributed over the planet's surface. Some regions receive high rainfall, while in deserts rain may not fall for years. Where water is scarce, people may have to spend hours every day just fetching enough to meet their needs. Elsewhere water may be plentiful, but purifying and distributing it still use up energy and cost money. Do you think it is important to save water? If so, can you think how it can be done?

SOIL PROFILE

Scientists distinguish several different layers called horizons in a vertical slice of soil, called a soil profile (right). The depth of each layer varies with the type of soil. The topmost layer (horizon O) is a rich layer of humus made of plant and animal remains. Below that the topsoil (horizon A) is a dark, fertile layer containing humus. The subsoil (horizon B) is nourished by minerals washed from the topsoil. The zone of partly weathered rock below that (horizon C) is less fertile. Last comes the bedrock (horizon D or R), the source of the minerals in the soil.

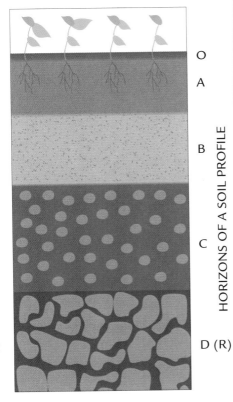

O
A
B
C
D (R)

HORIZONS OF A SOIL PROFILE

4 Ecosystems

Ecosystems are self-contained units made up of living things and their nonliving environment. An ecosystem can be as small as a tiny pool in a dry canyon or as vast as the ocean.

▼ *Even a small pool in a canyon, such as this one in Arizona, is an ecosystem.*

Luckily for us and all Earth's organisms, a number of factors come together to make our planet suitable for life. First, Earth is just the right distance from the sun to receive the light and heat needed for life to flourish. Earth's atmosphere protects us from harmful rays from space and contains life-giving oxygen. There is plenty of water, and the oceans as well as the atmosphere help regulate temperatures. In short, Earth has all the conditions needed to support life except an energy source, and that is provided by our local star, the sun.

THE BIOSPHERE, OR LIVING LAYER

The biosphere is all parts of Earth that are able to sustain life, including the atmosphere, oceans, the surface of the land, and just below it. This living layer extends from about 30,000 feet (9km) in the air down to the ocean depths and to about 8 miles (13km) below the land's surface, where microoogransims can survive. Above 30,000 feet the air is too thin to support life, while at depths greater than 8 miles the heat and the pressure are

LIVING PLANET

Some experts view the whole Earth as a single ecosystem because it is a self-contained unit that supports life. Indeed, some ecologists see Earth as a vast living organism (see 62–70). Our planet has remained in balance for millions of years and has a remarkable ability to recover from major disasters such as asteroid strikes and huge volcanic eruptions (see right). Many ecologists, however, are now concerned that human activities and pollution may soon upset the balance that sustains life on Earth.

In contrast, Mars is too far from the sun to sustain life. The average temperatures there, -16 °F (-23 °C), are too cold for life, since the atmosphere is too thin to retain heat. Venus, closer to the sun than we are, is too hot for life, with average temperatures of 480 °F (234 °C). Its thick, dense atmosphere has clouds of carbon dioxide. Also, neither of the planets Mars and Venus has enough water to support life.

BIOMES

Earth is divided into a number of huge ecosystems such as deserts, forests, tundra, and mountains. They fit together like the pieces of an enormous jigsaw puzzle. Each piece is a biome (see 33), with its own climate and distinctive soil, plants, and animals.

▼ *Living organisms exist in only a very small layer of Earth.*

too great. Within this living layer most life exists in a much narrower band, which extends from the sunlit upper waters of the oceans to about 1,000 feet (300m) in the air.

3,986 miles (6,400km) to center of Earth

ocean trench

Height to which life can exist in air: **30,000 feet (9km).**

Depth to which life can exist: **8 miles (13km).**

Depth to center of Earth: **3,986 miles (6,400km).**

TRY THIS

LOCAL ECOSYSTEMS

Make a map of the ecosystems in your area by tracing or photocopying a large-scale aerial photograph. Now survey the area on foot, noting ecosystems such as woodlands, ponds, fields, built-up areas, and wasteland. You could also mark particular features such as a rabbit or gopher warren or a colony of nesting birds.

Be very careful and ask an adult to go with you when you do the survey (see **1**: 38–47).

Some biomes support vast numbers of living organisms, while other biomes are much less productive. Of the dry land that occupies about 30 percent of Earth's surface, one-third is desert, and another fifth is either tundra (treeless areas where the sub-soil is frozen) or permanently covered with ice. These harsh biomes support relatively little life. Biomes such as forests, grasslands, and warm, shallow seas teem with life.

The climate, geography, and other factors allow certain types of vegetation to grow well. This in turn supports particular types of animals, fungi, and microscopic life.

The polar regions

The polar regions are the harshest places on Earth, with short, cold summers and long, dark, freezing winters. A desert is anywhere with less than 10 inches (25cm) of rain

▼ *Polar bears live in the Arctic. To keep out the cold, they have thick fur and a layer of fat.*

every year, so polar regions are deserts because there is very little rainfall and almost no liquid water on the ground. The land is permanently covered by a thick cap of ice more than 2 miles (3.2km) deep in places. The oceans are warmer but still frozen over for much of the year. Little life can survive on land in these bleak conditions; but the polar oceans, with their nutrient-rich currents, teem with life, from microscopic plankton to Earth's largest creatures, giant blue whales.

The tundras
The bleak, treeless lands that lie south of the arctic wastes are the tundra. There the climate is also harsh, with cool, brief summers and long, icy winters. Snow and ice cover the ground for much of the year, but in summer the snow melts to reveal grassy lowlands with bogs and lakes. Beneath the topsoil is a

layer of permanently frozen ground called the permafrost in which trees cannot root.

THE WORLD'S BIOMES

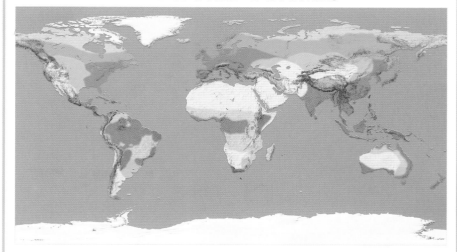

Biomes are large regions that have similar climate, plants, and animals. This map shows Earth's main land biomes: polar, tundra, mountain, desert, scrubland, grasslands, and forest. Forest biomes can be divided into cool, temperate, and tropical forests. Oceans and lakes offer saltwater and freshwater biomes. Each biome contains ecosystems with particular conditions. The distance from the equator is one factor that determines climate, so divisions between biomes broadly follow lines of latitude.

- Polar desert
- Arctic tundra
- Taiga
- Temperate forest
- Temperate grassland
- Desert and semidesert
- Shrubland
- Tropical grassland
- Tropical forest, including rainforest
- Mountain and highland
- Ocean

BUILDING ON THE TUNDRA

The harsh climate of the tundra makes the building of houses, roads, and other structures difficult. Engineers encounter problems because of the underlying permafrost. If heat is transferred to the frozen ground through a structure's foundations, the soil may become boggy, causing the structure to sink. If the ground freezes and thaws repeatedly, ice may heave up buildings, causing cracking. Many structures are built on stilts to avoid these problems. The Transalaska Pipeline, which transports oil mined in the arctic south across the tundra, has been built above ground to prevent the warm oil from melting the permafrost.

However, low-growing shrubs, mosses, lichens, and flowering plants make the most of the short summer growing season. Few animals live all year on the tundra. Insects die in the fall, leaving their eggs or larvae (young) in the soil to hatch the following spring. Birds and mammals that live year round include arctic foxes, lemmings, and snowy owls. Many more, including caribou, geese, ducks, and seabirds, migrate to the tundra to breed in spring.

Mountain biomes

The effects of altitude on climate (see 18–27) create mountain zones that contain several minibiomes with conditions similar to those normally encountered over a huge north–south range. The summits of high mountains are permanently covered with snow and ice, like the polar regions. Below that is a bleak, treeless zone with vegetation similar to the tundra. Farther down, lower slopes may feature cool forest and then

▼ *Mount Rainier and an alpine meadow in Mount Ranier National Park, Washington state. Mountain biomes vary from snowcapped peaks to temperate lower slopes, according to altitude.*

INTO THE PAST

THE AMERICAN DUST BOWL

In the 1930s bad farming practices turned a huge area of the American prairies into a barren wasteland. As the West was settled, farmers removed the natural vegetation to plant crops. Without grass roots to anchor the soil, year after year of drought reduced it to dust. High winds blew the dust away, creating a desert often called a dust bowl. The region's fertility was restored only after many years of careful management.

temperate or tropical plant life, depending on where the mountain is located.

Grasslands

Grasslands cover roughly 13 million square miles (34 square km) worldwide—about one-quarter of Earth's land area. Most grasslands lie between desert biomes and tropical or temperate forests. There are two main types of grasslands: savannas, or tropical grasslands, and temperate grasslands. Tropical grasslands generally experience an annual dry and rainy season, and have scattered trees and shrubs. Temperate grasslands receive a more even distribution of yearly rainfall.

The major temperate grasslands of the world include the Central Asian steppes and the American prairies. Huge tracts of these vast grasslands have been plowed to grow crops such as wheat, corn, and oats. Wild grasslands of the world are home to 7,500 different species of grasses but relatively few trees. Grasslands are rich biomes that support huge numbers of insects and microorganisms, and a variety of birds and reptiles. Grassland mammals fall in two main groups: burrowers and grazers. Burrowers include ground squirrels and rabbits, while grazers include antelope, zebras, and wildebeest.

▲ A 1930s dust-bowl farmer in Cimarron County, Oklahoma, raises a fence to keep it from being buried under drifting sand and dust. These dry wastelands were created when farmers cleared the land to plant their crops.

A deciduous, or seasonal, forest mostly made up of broad-leaved trees that shed their leaves in fall. This type of forest grows in temperate regions, which have warm summers and cool winters. The other two types of forests are coniferous and tropical.

Forest biomes

Forest biomes together cover over a quarter of Earth's land area. There are three main types of forests: coniferous, deciduous, and tropical forest. Climate is the main factor that determines which type of forest grows.

A wide belt of coniferous forest called the taiga rings the northern hemisphere south of the tundra. Conifers such as spruce, larch, fir, and pine thrive in the harsh climate there, with bitterly cold winters and low rainfall. These cone-bearing trees have narrow, waxy leaves that minimize moisture loss and withstand cold well. All except larch are evergreen. The dense foliage throughout the year severely limits the amounts of both light and moisture that filter through to ground level, so plant and animal life is relatively sparse on the forest floor.

The world's temperate regions are generally characterized by warm summers, cool winters, and abundant rainfall. Here forests of deciduous trees such as oak, beech,

APPLICATIONS

RAINFOREST PRODUCTS

Tropical forests yield hundreds of products familiar in stores in developed countries. Perhaps the most obvious is hardwood timber, used to make furniture. As well as a wide range of fruits, nuts, and spices, tropical forests also yield sugar, coffee, palm oil, chocolate, rubber, and chicle, ash, and maple shed their leaves in fall to conserve moisture in winter, then grow new leaves in spring. For much of the year the bare branches allow abundant light and moisture to reach the ground, where wildlife thrives in the rich soil. In tropical areas with an annual dry and rainy season trees also shed their leaves in the dry season.

Tropical rainforests grow in low-lying regions near the equator that receive more than 100 inches (250cm) of rain a year. Vegetation thrives in these warm, wet conditions and supports an abundance of wildlife. Rainforests cover just 6 percent of Earth's land area, yet scientists estimate they host up to 70 percent of all living species. The world's largest rainforest, the Amazon rainforest in South America, occupies a vast area. However tropical forests worldwide are disappearing at an alarming rate (see 50–61).

MAKE A MINI RAINFOREST

TRY THIS

Make a mini rainforest using an old fish tank or a large jar with a lid. Cover the base of the container with gravel, then add charcoal and a layer of compost. Plant tropical plants from a garden center in the soil, mist their leaves with a plant spray, and then replace the lid. The plants will recycle the moisture inside their mini-ecosystem, so you will not need to water them much.

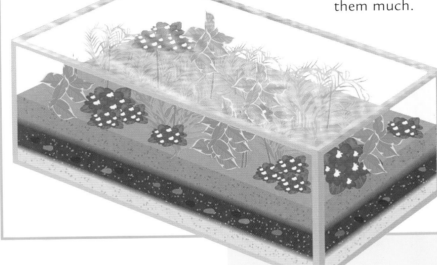

Desert and scrubland biomes

Deserts are defined as places where less than 10 inches (25cm) of rain falls annually. Scrublands, often on the

which is used to make chewing gum. In addition, plants such as the rosy periwinkle from Madagascar (right) are used to make medicines.

Joshua trees, cacti, and desert grasses growing in southwest Utah on the slopes of Beaver Dam Mountains. These species grow particularly well after wet winters.

borders of deserts, are slightly wetter but still have a low rainfall. In low-lying deserts, such as the Sahara Desert in Africa, temperatures may climb to 130 °F (54 °C) by day but drop steeply at night. High deserts such as the Gobi Desert in Central Asia have an even harsher climate, with temperatures that go below freezing at night.

Desert organisms have features that enable them to cope with the harsh conditions and particularly the lack of water. Many desert plants have a deep or extensive root system to gather moisture from the surrounding soil. Plants called succulents, such as cacti, store moisture in their fleshy leaves, stems, or roots. Many desert animals are active by night, when temperatures are cooler, and are able to withstand a period of drought.

Urban ecosystems

As human populations grow and expand around the world, so more and more wild land is transformed into urban environments. For many species this change is disastrous, but some types of plants and animals have adapted to thrive in this new habitat. Opportunistic feeders such as raccoons and foxes were once woodland species but now live in cities. Birds such as pigeons also do well in cities because they are able to exploit urban food sources.

EVOLUTION ON ISLANDS

The English naturalist Charles Darwin (1809–1882) visited the remote Galápagos Islands off Ecuador in the 1830s. His experiences there helped him formulate his ideas on evolution (see **9**: 16–25). He discovered many of the islands had their own species of birds called finches, with beaks specialized for different foods. Darwin speculated that all had evolved from a single species of finch that had reached the islands several hundred thousand years before.

Islands

Islands often have very different communities of plants and animals than the nearest mainland. The isolation of island habitats ensures that only certain species of plants and animals are able to reach and colonize them. Plants whose seeds are dispersed by wind and water, and flying animals such as birds, bats, and insects are common, but large, land-based predators are often absent. These conditions may cause island species to evolve along different lines than their mainland cousins. For example, many birds that have evolved on islands, such as New Zealand's kiwis, became flightless in the absence of predators. Island

▶ *A kiwi looks for food. These New Zealand birds are flightless and nocturnal (night active), searching out food at nighttime mainly by smell using their long, curved bills.*

▲ *Giraffes, zebras, and antelopes at a water hole in Namibia, Africa. These grazers and browsers eat slightly different plant foods, so they do not compete and can live in the same community.*

POPULATION ECOLOGY

In the wild, animal populations are held in balance by natural checks such as disease. In a particular year animal numbers may rise or fall, but they usually return to a consistent level over the course of several years. Competition for food among animals of the same species is one important factor. Different species within a community do not compete directly for food because they have different niches and eat slightly different foods.

Predator–prey relationships

In any ecosystem predators curb numbers of herbivores (plant eaters), and

species are especially vulnerable to changes in their environment, whether these changes occur naturally or if they are caused by humans (see 50–61).

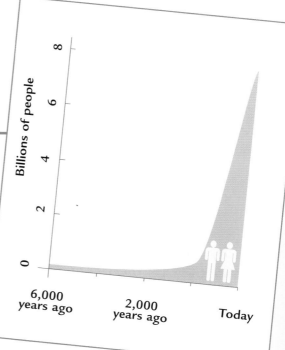

POPULATION EXPLOSION

HOT DEBATE

In contrast to animal populations, which do not usually keep rising, the number of people on Earth has risen steeply in the last few centuries (see right). Improved health care and more efficient farming practices mean that each year, more and more people live to an age at which they themselves can have children, so the human population "explodes." This huge increase puts great pressure on the natural resources on Earth and on ecosystems worldwide (see 50-61).

that in turn protects the plants at the base of the food chain. Many animal populations undergo a regular cycle of "boom and bust," which relates to factors such as climate. In years of harsh weather plant food is scarce, so herbivore and carnivore numbers remain low. In mild years plants thrive, and herbivores breed quickly. Increased numbers of prey prompt the predators to multiply; but when they become too numerous, populations of their prey may crash. Some predators starve, so their numbers drop, which allows the herbivores to recover. In this way balance is restored.

Territories

Many different types of animals, from fish to birds and mammals, establish group or individual territories. Each animal's "patch" contains enough food for the individual or group's needs, or is a safe place where the animals can breed or shelter. Animals defend their patch against others of their species, which limits the number of any one species a habitat will support. Animal territories thus help keep populations in balance.

Territory boundaries may be marked with scent or dung, or defined by audible calls or by visual shows of aggression. Animal territories vary greatly in size. For example, a pride of lions needs a huge territory in which to hunt, while seabirds such as common murres establish tiny territories on narrow cliff ledges just large enough for each bird to lay its eggs.

INTO THE PAST

HUMAN EXPANSION

In the 1800s the British economist Thomas Malthus (1766–1834) warned that human populations would expand very quickly unless checked by human-made or natural disasters such as war and disease. Charles Darwin, struck by Malthus's words, realized that animal and human populations were controlled by factors such as disease and competition. That helped him work out his famous theory of evolution by natural selection.

▶ *Some animals need larger territories to breed, feed, and shelter than others. Common murres are seabirds that need only very small territories like these nesting ledges (right) on which to lay their eggs.*

5 The Water World

▼ *An aerial view of a Mississippi delta town. The river splits into separate streams at the coast and dumps mud and other fine particles to form new land called a delta.*

Water covers 71 percent of Earth's surface. Aquatic ecosystems can be divided into fresh-water systems, such as lakes, rivers, and wetlands, and saltwater systems: seas and oceans. Semisalty, or brackish, waters are present in deltas, estuaries, and marshes, where fresh water mixes with the tide.

Four main factors affect the nature of aquatic ecosystems. They are salinity (salt content), oxygen levels, the amount of sunlight that reaches the water, and water temperature. Salinity is measured in parts per thousand (ppt). Seawater contains 35 to 70 ppt, fresh water only 15 to 30 ppt.

Sunlight penetrates only the upper waters of aquatic biomes. Moving waters such as swift-flowing streams and the surface of rough seas are particularly high in oxygen. The upper waters are also warmer than the depths, and water near the surface contains the most oxygen.

Marine ecosystems

The oceans are by far the largest biome on Earth. They occupy two-thirds of the planet's surface and support an estimated 250,000 species of living organisms. Marine organisms can be divided into three groups, of which one is plankton—generally, small creatures and microorganisms that float on the water. The other groups are larger, actively swimming creatures, including fish, squid, and marine mammals; and smaller,

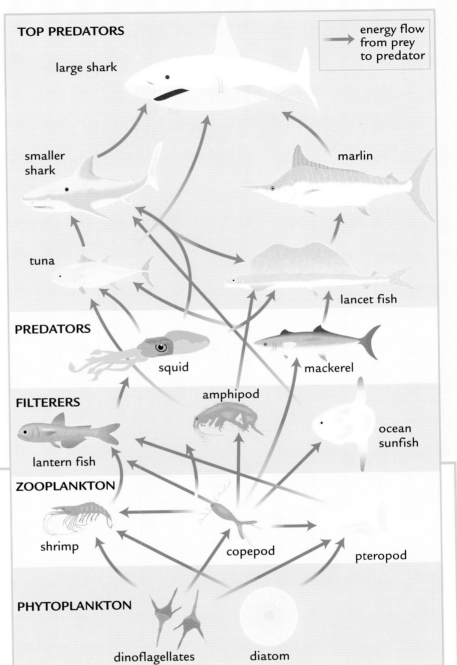

TOP PREDATORS

energy flow from prey to predator

large shark

smaller shark

marlin

tuna

lancet fish

PREDATORS

squid

mackerel

amphipod

FILTERERS

ocean sunfish

lantern fish

ZOOPLANKTON

shrimp

copepod

pteropod

PHYTOPLANKTON

dinoflagellates

diatom

AQUATIC FOOD WEBS

Almost all life in aquatic habitats depends on the sun for energy, as on land. Aquatic food webs are as vast and complex as land-based webs. At the base of the food chain tiny plantlike, single-celled algae called phytoplankton floating at the surface harness the sun's energy through photosynthesis (see **5**: 6–13). In so doing, the phytoplankton produce a surprising 70 percent of the world's oxygen. Tiny animals called zooplankton feed on the phytoplankton and, in turn, provide food for larger creatures, and so on up the food chain. In the oceans small crustaceans called copepods and krill, part of the zooplankton, are food for the largest creatures, baleen whales. When aquatic organisms die, their remains are eaten either by scavengers such as shrimp and crabs or by microorganisms. The microorganisms break down organic remains into simpler compounds so their energy can be recycled.

OCEAN HARVEST

APPLICATIONS

The oceans have always been a rich source of food for people and also for marine and shore predators. Since prehistoric times people of coastal regions worldwide have used nets, lines, and harpoons to harvest fish and other marine life.

In the last 100 years or so, fishing methods have become so efficient that fish populations have dropped steeply.

Governments of fishing nations now set strict quotas to control the numbers of fish that can be caught, in an attempt to let fish stocks recover.

less active creatures, including starfish, corals, sea anemones, sea lilies, and sponges that live on the bottom of the ocean.

Marine ecosystems can be divided into two main biomes: the deep ocean and the tidal zone—the shallow waters that edge the coasts. Tidal zone biomes include coral reefs, which are sometimes compared to rainforests because they support a huge diversity of life. In addition, there are shoreline ecosystems and semisalty habitats such as deltas and estuaries.

The deep, open ocean can be divided into vertical zones that can be compared to the vertical layers called stories that divide forest ecosystems (see 8). There are three main zones: the sunlit zone, the

▲ *Coral reefs are built from layer upon layer of the chalky calcium carbonate skeletons of marine animals called coral polyps, or corals.*

midwater, and the deep. Life is present at all depths of the ocean, but the sunlit upper waters are very productive and have the most biomass (amount of living material).

Upper waters
Plants and algae, including seaweeds, grow only in the sunlit upperwaters of the ocean or in coastal shallows on the seabed. In spring the phytoplankton multiply, or "bloom," in response to the longer hours of daylight, creating an abundance of food for herbivores (plant eaters).

OCEAN ZONES

The sunlit upper waters, called the euphotic zone, extend to a depth of 650 feet (195m). Beyond that lies the midwater zone, which extends to about 6,500 feet (1,950m). The upper waters of the midwater are sometimes called the twilight zone since some light reaches here, but no light penetrates below 3,000 feet (900m) to the region called the dark zone. The deep-sea zone lies below 6,500 feet and may include ocean trenches descending to 35,000 feet (10,500m). Each zone is home to a distinctive community of organisms; however, deep-diving creatures such as sperm whales regularly move between the zones.

Some free-swimming creatures, including filter-feeding baleen whales, migrate long distances to feast on phytoplankton—or on herbivores.

Many fish of the upper waters, such as mackerel and herring, have dark backs and pale bellies. This coloration, termed countershading, helps conceal them both from seabirds hunting in the air above and from predators below. The seabirds cannot easily see the fish while looking toward the darkness of the water from above, nor can the ocean predators see the fish while looking toward the light from below.

Bottom dwellers

The ocean floor is as varied as the surface of the land, with features such as high ridges, tall peaks called seamounts, vast plains, and deep trenches. Bottoms may be rocky, sandy, or in the case of many deep oceans, covered with a layer of

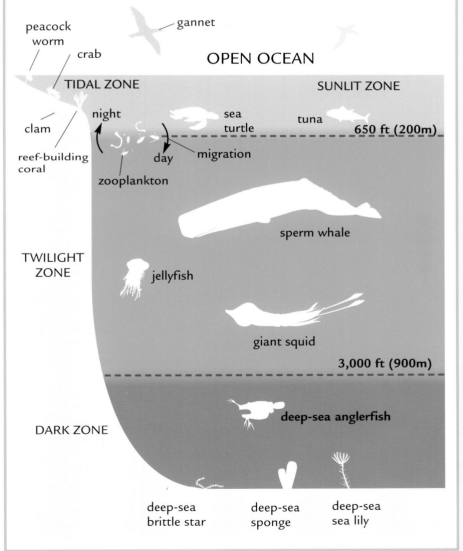

OPEN OCEAN

peacock worm · gannet · crab · night · clam · reef-building coral · zooplankton · day · migration · TIDAL ZONE · sea turtle · tuna · SUNLIT ZONE · 650 ft (200m) · sperm whale · TWILIGHT ZONE · jellyfish · giant squid · 3,000 ft (900m) · DARK ZONE · deep-sea anglerfish · deep-sea brittle star · deep-sea sponge · deep-sea sea lily

MONSTERS OF THE DEEP

In past times people believed the ocean depths were the home of huge, monstrous creatures.
One such creature was the kraken, a legendary, many-armed beast that rose from the depths to drag ships to their doom. This legend is now thought to have been inspired by giant deep-sea squid. With the rise of science such superstitions faded. About 150 years ago scientists believed nothing could exist in the deep. Now we know monstrous-looking deep-sea fish do exist, but are rarely more than 1 foot (30cm) long.

silty ooze. Plaice, rays, and other bottom-dwelling fish are adapted to their habitat with wide, flattened bodies for moving along the seabed. Some deep-sea creatures, such as sea spiders and the extraordinary tripod fish, have long legs or leglike spines that act as stilts and hold the animals high above the ooze.

Wildlife of the depths

Food is scarce in the dark ocean depths. Fish and other deep-sea creatures feed on plant and animal remains that drift down from the waters above or prey on one another. Fish such as gulper eels and viperfish have huge jaws, sharp teeth, and stretchy stomachs so they can make

UNDERSEA EXPLORATION

The ocean depths were one of the last places on Earth to be explored because of the great difficulties of deep undersea exploration. Submarines were developed in the 1870s, but they could not make deep dives. In 1934 U.S. naturalists Charles Beebe (1877–1962) and Otis Barton (1899–1992)

descended to 2,500 feet (750m) in a submarine called a bathysphere. In the 1960s Swiss naturalist Jacques Piccard (born 1922) reached the deepest point in the oceans, the Mariana Trench in the Pacific, in a craft called a bathyscaphe. The Japanese

bathyscaphe *Kaiko* explored the Mariana Trench in the 1990s.
The U.S. Navy-owned deep submergence vehicle (DSV) *Alvin* (above) has been used for ocean research since 1964. An eight-hour dive can take two scientists and a pilot to a depth of 14,764 feet (4,500m).

the most of any prey they come across. Some deep-sea animals can swallow creatures twice their own size.

In the twilight zone, where dim light penetrates, some fish have rows of little lights on their bellies to disguise their shadow. The light may be produced either by special organs called photophores or by luminous (light-emitting) bacteria in the fish's skin.

In the deep oceans scientists discovered clams and tubeworms living around hydrothermal vents. These vents are cracks or chimneys from which black, billowing clouds of superhot, sulfur-rich water well up from inside Earth's crust.

The clams and worms do not depend on sunlight to make their food but get all their nutrients from bacteria inside their bodies. In turn, the bacteria get energy to make food from the sulfur present in the hydrothermal vents.

▲ *A vent called a black smoker on the midocean ridge, an undersea chain of mountains. The deep submergence vehicle (DSV) Alvin discovered vents in 1974.*

▼ *A moray eel hides in a crack on the ocean floor. Moray eels live in warm seas and are predators that have sharp teeth.*

APPLICATIONS

EXPLOITING THE OCEANS

As well as seafood, the oceans yield many other useful products, including precious pearls and minerals such as manganese, which covers some parts of the seabed. The oceans also provide energy. For example, oil and natural gas can be mined from the seabed, and the power of waves and tides can be harnessed to produce electricity. Seawater can even provide fresh drinking water if the salt is removed, but this process is expensive.

REEFS AT RISK

Coral reefs are the ocean's richest habitats, yet these amazing structures are now under threat throughout warm oceans. Pollution is one of the main dangers. Sewage from seaside towns and chemicals from farms and factories pollute the clear waters in which the polyps live. In some areas the coral is being mined to provide building materials or divers break off bits of reef as souvenirs. Global warming (see 25) produces warmer seas, so is a danger because coral polyps are very sensitive to temperature change.

TRY THIS
EXPLORING POOL LIFE

Each pool on the beach is a mini-ecosystem. What can you find out about life in a pool on the nearest shore? First, is the beach sandy, rocky, or shingly? Is the pool situated on the upper, middle, or lower shore? Now analyze the pool itself. Is it deep? Do you think the water is very salty, or does it contain rainwater? Can you see any plants or seaweed? Now try to spot herbivores such as limpets and periwinkles, predators such as dog whelks, and scavengers such as shrimp and crabs. Can you draw a food web connecting theorganisms you see?

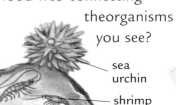

sea urchin

shrimp

▲ *Many types of fish live in and around coral reefs because there is plenty of food and lots of safe places in which to hide.*

SAFETY NOTE   If you go to the beach, be very careful near water or rocks. Don't touch animals or plants. Ask an adult to go with you.

seaweed

COASTAL AND INTERTIDAL ZONES
Coral reefs

Coral reefs are present only in warm, shallow waters off tropical coasts. The reefs are made of the chalky skeletons of millions of small, sea anemonelike reef-building corals called coral polyps that build up on top of one another over thousands of years. Some coral reefs are 40–50 million years old and are made up of coral three-quarters of a mile (1.2km) thick. The world's largest coral reef, Australia's Great Barrier Reef, stretches over 1,240 miles (2,000km) and can be seen from space. In places it towers 500 feet (150m) above the seabed. Coral reefs occupy only a small fraction of coastal waters worldwide, but these ecosystems support an estimated 25 percent of marine life, providing food, shelter, and hundreds of hiding places for many creatures. For instance, one of the reefs at Key Largo, Florida, has more than 550 species.

Seashores

Worldwide, there are more than over 300,000 miles (480,000km) of coastline. Rocky, shingly, sandy, and muddy beaches each host their own communities of life. Rocky shores are rich in wildlife, including seaweeds, barnacles, shrimps, limpets, sea anemones, and crabs. Cockles, clams, and razor

SEASHORE ZONES

Seashores are divided into three zones between the high- and low-tide mark: the upper, middle, and lower shore. Each is home to distinctive plants, animals, and other life. Beyond the upper zone lies the splash zone, where rocks are misted by salt spray and stained with lichen. Limpets, periwinkles, barnacles, shrimp, and wrack seaweeds are present on the upper and middle shore. Lobsters, sea anemones, sea urchins, kelp, and fish such as lumpfish thrive in pools on the lower shore.

HIGH LEVEL: upper shore and splash zone

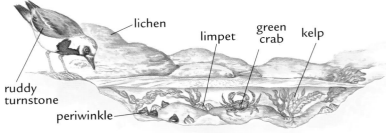

lichen — limpet — green crab — kelp — ruddy turnstone — periwinkle

MIDLEVEL: middle shore

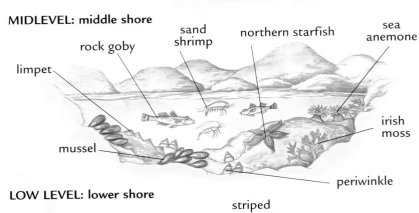

rock goby — sand shrimp — northern starfish — sea anemone — limpet — irish moss — mussel — periwinkle

LOW LEVEL: lower shore

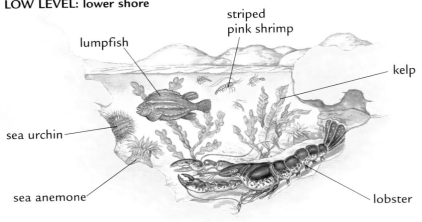

lumpfish — striped pink shrimp — kelp — sea urchin — sea anemone — lobster

CLOSEUP

OXYGEN LEVELS AND POLLUTION

The levels of oxygen in freshwater habitats are affected by pollution, which can harm local wildlife. Fertilizers used in farming contain nutrients. Water drained from fields makes freshwater systems superrich in nutrients, which causes algae and bacteria to multiply. Algae blanket the water surface (see below) and block sunlight from plants that produce oxygen. As algae die, oxygen-consuming microorganisms eat the algae and use up lots of oxygen. As a result, fish and other wildlife suffocate.

shells live on sandy beaches. Many sandy-beach animals burrow for protection from predators and so as not to dry out when the tide is out.

Seashores are harsh habitats, where conditions are continuously changing. The animals and plants living there spend part of each day covered by water and the remainder exposed to the weather, which may be baking sunshine, winds, or rain. Organisms have to adapt to these two different lifestyles. They time their resting and feeding periods to match the rhythm of the tides.

FRESHWATER ECOSYSTEMS

Fresh water covers only a small part of Earth's surface but offers a range of habitats. Freshwater ecosystems may be divided into still-water systems, such as lakes, ponds, swamps, and marshes, and habitats with flowing

USES OF WETLANDS

Rivers, lakes, and other bodies of fresh water have countless uses. Most important, they supply water for wildlife and also for human settlements, farming, and industry. Around the world many settlements are located by rivers, lakes, and other wetlands or on the coast. Wetlands act as reservoirs and also help prevent flooding after heavy rain has fallen by soaking up excess water. They also provide a wealth of food from fish, shellfish, and waterfowl to fruit and crops such as rice. Aquatic mammals such as otters and muskrats once yielded valuable fur for clothing. Timber and materials like rushes, traditionally used in roofing (below), also come from wetlands.

water, namely, rivers and streams. As in the oceans, the productivity of freshwater habitats is affected by many factors. These factors include soil type, water depth, water temperature, sunlight and oxygen levels, minerals, and pollution. Freshwater habitats rich in nutrients and organic matter are also rich in life. Wetlands fed by water from acidic rocks or peaty ground are low in nutrients.

BUILD A MINIPOND

Build a minipond in your backyard using an old washbowl or a piece of plastic sheeting. First, ask your parents to help choose a good site for the pond. Dig a bowl-shaped hollow with a spade or trowel, place the bowl or plastic sheeting inside, then firm the soil back around the edge. Cover the bottom with a layer of gravel, then put stones around the edge and on the bottom. Add water plants, and fill the pond with water. It won't be long until wildlife begins to colonize (move into) the pond.

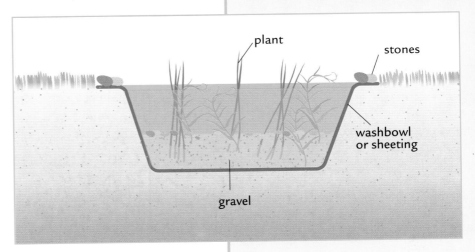

plant

stones

washbowl or sheeting

gravel

6 Human Impacts

Over the last few centuries people have spread to every part of Earth and transformed many landscapes. As human numbers increase, we put more and more pressure on the natural world.

Modern human civilization began about 9,000 years ago as people began to grow crops in parts of the Middle East and, somewhat later, Egypt, northern India, and China. Settlements grew up in places where people could find food and water, and also safety from their enemies. Farmers learned to irrigate the land so crops could be grown. New techniques and machinery gradually made

▼ Farmers in this part of South Africa have planted just one type of crop, a practice called monoculture. To carry out this type of farming, they kill off all the wild plants.

farming ever more efficient. Now many modern crop fields are "green deserts" where just one plant, the crop, is nurtured at the expense of wild plants and insect life, which farmers poison with pesticides and herbicides.

From the 1790s the Industrial Revolution saw the start of modern manufacturing methods. Now factories are built all over the world. Modern industries use up huge amounts of energy and natural resources, and produce considerable pollution (see 56–61). And in the last 20 years the human population has mushroomed. In 1980 there were about 4 billion people on Earth; by 2000 there were 6 billion. Experts think there may be 9 billion by 2050. This puts a huge strain on natural resources and the environment.

Habitat destruction

One of the main effects of the growing number of people on Earth is habitat destruction, as people take over the natural habitats where wild species once lived. Every year

INTO THE PAST

NEW TOWN

More than 8,000 years ago one of the world's oldest towns, Çatal Höyük, existed in what is now Turkey near a range of hills where a hard volcanic stone called obsidian was mined. It was used to make tools and weapons, and was also traded. Many of the world's first settlements sprang up to exploit natural resources like this. In the Middle East, Egypt, India, and China the first major cities grew up on the banks of rivers that provided transportation, water, and protection against enemy attacks.

HOT DEBATE

SPRAWLING CITIES

Many cities founded just a few centuries ago are now huge. The world's biggest cities include Mexico City, Sao Paolo in Brazil, Seoul in South Korea, Tokyo (right), Moscow, London, and New York. In overcrowded cities hygiene, sewage management, and even getting clean water may be a problem, particularly in developing countries. More than half the world's population now lives in cities.

▲ A green turtle covers its eggs in the sands of Ascension Island, South Atlantic Ocean. Care must be taken to stop tourists from disrupting such important wildlife activities.

more and more wild land is plowed just to grow enough food for people or to graze domestic livestock. Over-grazed land is prone to erosion; the animals eat or trample everything, including the roots that hold together the soil. Huge areas of land also disappear under concrete as new towns and industrial parks spring up, and roads, railroads, and powerlines are blazed through forests, deserts, and wildernesses.

In many parts of the world governments are handing over wild land to mining companies to dig or drill for minerals and fuel, or to construction firms to build dams to produce hydroelec-tric power. The tourist indus-try also puts increasing pres-sure on wild areas such as mountain regions, coral reefs, and sandy beaches. Many people like to "get back to

CLOSEUP

VANISHING WETLANDS

Around the world natural wetlands are disappearing fast. They are being drained to provide land for farming or new sites for factories and towns. Rivers and other freshwater systems are mined for gold and gemstones, building materials such as sand and gravel, or fuels such as peat. Some wetlands also disappear as they dry or silt up naturally, or when the land subsides. The United States has lost half its wetlands since the start of European settlement. Two-thirds of Europe's wetlands have vanished in the last 300 years.

RAINFOREST DESTRUCTION

Tropical rainforests contain the greatest biodiversity of any habitat on Earth. Experts estimate that around two-thirds of all species live there. However, this precious habitat is also disappearing faster than any other. Tropical rainforests now occupy less than half the area they did just a century ago. These forests are being felled for their valuable hardwood timber or for fuel and to clear land to grow crops and ranch cattle (right). Mining and dam building are also nibbling away at forests in some areas. This problem is called deforestation.

Destruction of rainforests harms the balance of gases in the atmosphere and affects the world's climate. Forest trees absorb carbon dioxide and so increase oxygen levels in the atmosphere. Felled trees can no longer take in carbon dioxide or release oxygen.

In addition, if the forests are burned to clear the land, carbon is released, adding to levels of carbon dioxide in the atmosphere. Since carbon dioxide is a greenhouse gas (see 18–27), deforestation contributes to the problem of global warming—rising temperatures worldwide.

nature" on vacation, yet sprawling resorts can spoil the scenery that tourists come to enjoy. Large numbers of visitors can disturb wildlife such as turtles nesting on beaches.

EXTINCT WOLVES

Tasmanian wolves were unusual marsupials that lived only on the island of Tasmania off Australia. From the 1800s European settlers hunted them because they occasionally took sheep and poultry. With their tigerlike stripes these "wolves" were reputed to be fierce creatures, but were in fact no bigger than dogs. They also had fatal diseases and the last one died in Hobart zoo in 1936, so the "wolf" is now extinct.

A skeleton of a Tasmanian wolf, with a model in the background. These animals were hunted and are now extinct.

Overhunting

As human numbers have risen, overexploitation of the world's wildlife has become a major problem. For thousands of years people have hunted animals on land and in rivers and oceans for meat and also for hides, fur, or feathers. When the human population was smaller, this hunting did little harm. In recent centuries the invention of guns, explosive harpoons, and devices such as sonar, used to detect fish, have made the killing much easier. Overhunting and overfishing now threaten the survival of many ocean and land species.

In addition to hunting for food, dangerous animals such as tigers, sharks, and snakes are often hounded because people fear them as killers. Elephants, rhinoceroses, and big cats are killed, often illegally, for their ivory or fur. Elsewhere animals as diverse as monkeys, parrots, and

WHALING

The European whaling industry began around 1600. Throughout the 1700s, 1800s, and early 1900s whales were hunted relentlessly for their meat, oil, bones, and baleen (hornlike material on the upper jaw). By 1950 many of the once-numerous great whales were almost extinct.

In the 1990s some whaling was banned by many nations. Now that the slaughter has ended, many whale populations have begun to recover.

terrapins are threatened by the pet trade. Animals that are captured in the wild rarely survive long in captivity. In the past, overhunting killed off species such as the dodo (see **9**: 53). Ecologists fear that many more species may soon go the same way.

Introduced species

Every ecosystem on Earth has its own community of plants, animals, and other organisms suited to that particular environment. The introduction of new species to an area can upset the natural balance of life there. All over the world people have brought in new, nonnative plants and animals to provide food, to control native species seen as pests (see right), or simply to improve the scenery. If the new arrivals then thrive and multiply, they can quickly crowd out and threaten the original native species there (see 28–39).

UNWELCOME ADDITION

In the 1930s a panel of experts recommended that the cane toad of Central America (below) should be introduced to Australia to control beetle pests in the sugar cane plantations there.

These amphibians were duly brought to Australia and released. Unfortunately, the large, poisonous toads bred quickly and now threaten native frogs, reptiles, and even small mammals.

Pollution

Pollution means any form of contamination of land, air, or water often caused by people. It may be deliberate or happen accidentally. Pollution is spread though the air by winds, by currents in moving water, and through the soil by seeping groundwater. Once in the ecosystem the contamination is absorbed by wildlife at a point in the food chain and passes up through the chain as carnivores eat herbivores. Top predators that feed on large numbers of polluted prey are sometimes the most contaminated of all. In the early 1960s, for example, the American bald eagle nearly died out because pesticide concentrations built up in its prey and thus within the eagles' own bodies. As a result, their eggshells became too fragile for the eggs to survive.

Human activities such as mining, manufacturing, energy production, and farming produce substantial amounts of pollution. So does the waste we produce daily in our homes, offices, and schools.

▼ *Smog caused by burning coal pollutes the air over Xian, China. Burning fossil fuels like coal and oil releases poisonous vapors into the atmosphere.*

Fossil fuels (oil, gas, and coal) burned in factories, power plants, and cars release toxic fumes into the atmosphere. Car exhausts spew out carbon dioxide, carbon monoxide, and sometimes lead. Devices called catalytic converters can reduce this pollution. These poisonous gases are a major cause of the dirty smog that hangs in the air over cities, causing breathing problems.

Rivers, lakes, and oceans are polluted by chemicals from factories and by fertilizers and pesticides used in farming. The soil is poisoned by chemicals from industry, mining, and agriculture, and also by the disposal of waste in sites called landfills. The problem of how to deal with all the waste we produce in our homes and factories gets bigger each year.

CLOSEUP

THE CHERNOBYL DISASTER

In 1986 one of the world's worst-ever pollution disasters was caused by an accident at a nuclear power plant. The nuclear reactor at Chernobyl in Ukraine, USSR, caught fire and exploded. A huge cloud of radioactive gas escaped and was spread over a vast area by the wind (below). In Scandinavia and Siberia tundra vegetation was contaminated, which poisoned wildlife such as reindeer. Thousands of deer had to be destroyed.

TRY THIS

MONITORING WATER POLLUTION

The presence of certain aquatic creatures in streams and rivers gives clues about the water quality. Caddisfly and mayfly larvae and freshwater shrimp thrive only in water that is clean. See if these creatures can be found in a stream or pond near you. Take care not to get too close to the edge and fall in. Use a net to sweep the water, then transfer your catch to a bowl while you identify the species using a field guide. Return the minibeasts to the water after you have finished looking at them.

POLLUTION IN THE POLAR REGIONS

The polar regions are generally far from major towns and industrial centers that release pollution. However, they are rich in minerals that can cause contamination of both the land and the sea. In the Arctic mining and drilling for gold, uranium, lead, coal, oil, and natural gas have caused considerable pollution on land and in the water. The Antarctic is also rich in minerals, but the continent is a wildlife sanctuary, so no mining is allowed there. However, traces of pollution from distant sources, such as radioactive contamination from Chernobyl, have been found in the Antarctic ice.

Ocean pollution

For centuries oceans have been used as a dumping ground for sewage and all types of dangerous chemicals. A staggering 20 million tons of rubbish are dumped in the oceans every year, including huge items of junk such as discarded oil rigs. Coastal waters are often the most heavily polluted because pipes discharge raw sewage and chemicals into the shallows. Filter-feeders and scavengers such as mollusks and crustaceans absorb the pollution and are then eaten by fish and other predators. Researchers in the Arctic have monitored pollution levels in top predators such as polar bears that feed on fish and seals. Some of the bears contained so much poison they could be classed as toxic waste.

Pollution-related hazards

Pollution of the air, water, and land has led to a number of very serious environmental problems. One of them is global warming, caused by the increase in greenhouse gases in the atmosphere partly due to burning fossil fuels (see 18–27). The warmer weather causes ice in the polar regions to melt. If this continues,

ACID RAIN

Acid rain is a form of pollution that results when nitrogen oxide from car exhausts and sulfur dioxide from power plants enter the atmosphere. These gases mix with water vapor in the air to form weak acids, which then fall as rain. Acid rain can kill trees, harm wildlife, and eat away at buildings (right).

▶ *A sea otter tries to shake oil off its fur after the Exxon Valdez accident, in which hundreds of tons of oil spilled into Prince William Sound, Alaska. Thousands of animals were killed, and it took workers years to clean up the area.*

rising sea levels may threaten low-lying coastal regions, such as Louisiana, Bangladesh, and The Netherlands. Ozone loss in the atmosphere, caused by polluting chemicals called CFCs (see 23), means that more harmful ultraviolet radiation reaches Earth.

Oil spills

Oil spills are a major source of marine pollution. One of the worst-ever oil spills affected a huge area of Arctic coast. In 1989 the Exxon oil tanker *Valdez* ran aground off Prince William Sound in Alaska, spilling 50,000 tons of oil into the sea. More than 1,200 miles (1,900km) of coastline were polluted, and thousands of birds, sea otters, fish, and shellfish died. The disaster cost billions of dollars to clean up.

Minimizing human impact

What can be done to reduce pollution and other damage to the natural world? The

GREENHOUSE GASES

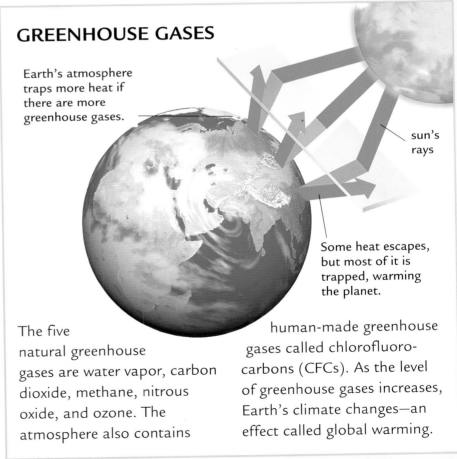

Earth's atmosphere traps more heat if there are more greenhouse gases.

sun's rays

Some heat escapes, but most of it is trapped, warming the planet.

The five natural greenhouse gases are water vapor, carbon dioxide, methane, nitrous oxide, and ozone. The atmosphere also contains human-made greenhouse gases called chlorofluorocarbons (CFCs). As the level of greenhouse gases increases, Earth's climate changes—an effect called global warming.

INTO THE PAST

TIMELY WARNING

In the 1960s the pioneering U.S. ecologist Rachel Carson (1907–1964) warned of the dangers of a pesticide called DDT, which poisoned wildlife. In her book *Silent Spring* she predicted that use of chemicals such as DDT in agriculture would eventually lead to a world barren of wildlife, where no birds sang. Carson's campaign eventually succeeded, and the deadly chemical was banned in the United States.

effects of habitat destruction can be reduced by creating sanctuaries and reserves where no development is allowed. Building on brown field sites—empty ground in city centers—can preserve wild habitats on the edge of towns.

Replanting can restore lost forests, and careful management of land can prevent erosion. Organic farming, in which farmers avoid chemical fertilizers and pesticides and rely on traditional methods such as crop rotation, can minimize the impact of farming on the environment. The major cause of pollution and habitat destruction is the human population explosion.

It can be curbed by more effective birth control.

Governments around the world are introducing laws to control the release of chemicals by cities, industry, and agriculture. Cooperation is needed to tackle ozone loss and global warming. Many countries have agreed not to use CFCs, which cause ozone loss. Governments have met to agree on targets to reduce greenhouse gas emissions.

▼ *Workers harvest lettuce on an organic farm. Organic farmers do not use artificial fertilizers and pesticides, and so reduce the harmful effect of agriculture on the environment.*

Development of renewable energy sources such as solar, wind, and water power can slow down global warming. People can tackle pollution by using less energy and chemicals and reducing waste.

▼ *An ecotourist walks through a tropical rainforest in Daintree National Park, Queensland, Australia. Limiting visitors to certain areas stops them from harming the wildlife and their habitats.*

WILDLIFE TOURISM

In many parts of the world ecotourism now helps protect wildlife. Ecotourists pay to see wildlife in natural surroundings such as reserves. Their money helps pay for the park upkeep and for local conservation programs.

Ecotourism helps the conservation work in reserves worldwide, such as Australia's Great Barrier Reef, in the wilds of Antarctica, and in Nepal's Annapurna mountain sanctuary.

SAVING ENERGY AND RECYCLING

We can all tackle the problems of global warming and acid rain by saving energy and recycling household waste. Think about ways in which your family or school could save energy. Switching off lights and machines when they are not needed, turning down the central heating, and making compost from vegetable peelings can help. So can using the car less. Note all the car journeys your family makes in a week. Are they all necessary, or could you walk, cycle, or take public transportation instead? Taking old cans, bottles, paper, and plastic packaging to recycling centers so they can be used again reduces waste. Use fewer chemicals and fertilizers on lawns.

7 Conservation

Children looking at a tidal rock pool. Many different types of living organisms inhabit such an ecosystem. It is important to carefully preserve these types of natural resources.

Conservation is the action taken by people to protect and preserve the natural world and its resources, such as living organisms, to prevent them from going extinct and losing valuable species forever.

Generally, people agree that natural resources should not be used up or wasted, but they may have different views about what makes a good conservation plan for a particular region. People often disagree about the right balance between environmental interests and economic ones. Sometimes scientists think that a habitat should be preserved and protected but differ on how

people should use the area. For example, someone who visits a national park to relax or enjoy listening to animal sounds does not appreciate someone else who uses a snowmobile or motorized all-terrain vehicle there. People who participate in bird watching or hiking activities do not want to do so at the same time that others are hunting wild game. A major role of conservation biologists is to settle such conflicts.

People who try to preserve the natural world (conservationists) believe it is very important to look after the land and water as well as living organisms. Sometimes the best conservation plan to protect a habitat is to limit the number of people allowed in and let the ecosystem operate naturally.

▲ Hunters in South Africa searching for wild game. Big game hunting must be controlled to ensure that species such as tigers and rhinoceroses are not pushed into extinction.

Basic principles

Conservation biologists consider three basic principles for developing a conservation plan. First, that evolutionary change (see **9**: 4–7) is a basic process in any living system. All species in natural ecosystems respond to environmental

---

CLOSEUP

THE AMERICAN BISON

Millions of American bison, or buffalo, once roamed the open plains of North America. Many Native American peoples depended on them for food, clothing, and shelter. In 1830 the government began killing the bison to control the Native Americans. By 1900 fewer than 1,000 bison were left, and conservationists worked hard to save them.

history. Long-term conservation plans that involve changing and managing habitats need to consider differences in the life styles of various living organisms as a consequence of their evolutionary past. Many insects, small mammals, and native grasses live no longer than a year, while freshwater turtles, tortoises, and oak trees grow for several years before becoming adults, maturing and then producing offspring.

A beaver building a dam can affect other species nearby.

change, so conservation plans must consider how species can respond based on their

The second principle is that the environment is always changing because of factors

HOW CONSERVATION BEGAN

Several centuries after the colonization of North America by Europeans people began to realize that natural resources were limited and could be used up by activities such as clearing forests and building towns, cities, and factories. In the 19th century the writer Henry David Thoreau (1817–1862) promoted an idea called the romantic-transcendental conservation ethic (a harmonious appreciation of and coexistence with nature). During the same century the naturalist John Muir (1838–1914) helped form the Sierra Club, which encouraged people to enjoy, learn about, and preserve natural settings. His efforts contributed to the creation of several national parks, including Yosemite.

The resource conservation ethic, promoted by forester named Gifford Pinchot, was based directly on economics and commercial interests. Pinchot believed that natural resources, including forests, should be used to produce materials for human use. This viewpoint led to a type of forest management in which commercial markets were built into the conservation plan so that timber production, mining, hunting, and fishing were balanced against habitat and wildlife preservation.

The most scientific approach to conservation, the evolutionary-ecological land ethic, was developed by the naturalist Aldo Leopold (1887–1948) in the early 20th century. Leopold viewed natural ecosystems as complex, interworking parts. Most scientists engaged in conservation programs support many of these views.

Modern approaches to conservation combine the three ethics identified above.

such as weather, season, and species interactions. Modern conservation biologists do not expect the pattern of distribution and the number of plant and animal species in an area to remain the same. This principle goes against an earlier concept that nature is in a balanced state.

Conservation plans should be based on an understanding that the types of species and population levels always change. For example, if beavers move into an area with a small stream, they usually build dams that make ponds that might attract some species, such as wading birds. Decreasing the stream flow might result in there being a reduction in certain other species, such as stream-side salamanders.

The third and final principle of any conservation plan is human society. Human needs and preferences can easily cause conflict and disagreement. There are situations in which conservation biologists must think about the needs or desires of the original inhabitants of a region. For example, conservation plans to preserve and protect natural habitats in Australia now include the attitudes and feelings of the aboriginal peoples, who are the original Australian inhabitants. Also, the International Whaling Commission (IWC) has a quota (allowance) for the hunting of bowhead whales. This permits Alaskan Inuits and the native people of Chukotka, Russia, to follow their cultural traditions of whale hunting.

HOT DEBATE

GAIA HYPOTHESIS

In the 1960s British scientist James Lovelock (born 1919) published the Gaia Hypothesis. It is the idea that Earth's oceans, atmosphere, and landmasses are held in equilibrium (balance) by all the living organisms of the planet, including humans. The hypothesis is that the living world operates like a superorganism, keeping a worldwide environmental balance. Not all scientists agree with the idea.

▼ *Inuit whalers landing a bowhead whale. Conservation plans are built around the Inuits' whale-hunting customs.*

ROAD KILLS AND LOSS OF HABITAT

Loss of habitat is one of the greatest threats to animals in most countries, and highways are a major cause. In the United States highways take up around 1 percent of the land surface, and about one million animals are killed on the roads every day. By noting the number of road-killed animals in an area, particularly after a highway has been newly built, conservationists can find out how badly natural habitats are affected and help make people aware of the importance of finding ways to prevent as many animals as possible from being killed in this way.

Ecological reserves

One of the greatest threats to biodiversity and ecosystems is the destruction of habitats. Conservation programs have resulted in the establishment of ecological reserves that protect species from human activities and allow them to live in these regions. Many countries have put aside land, freshwater, seashore, and marine habitats as national parks and wildlife refuges for the protection of living organisms.

One of the most successful U.S. conservation approaches

▼ *Setting aside areas as national parks, such as Yellowstone National Park (below), helps protect living organisms.*

ever taken was the setting aside of natural lands as national parks. Yellowstone National Park in the western United States, established by Congress in 1872, was the world's first national park. Royal National Park near Sydney, Australia, established in 1879, became the second.

Many countries in Africa, Europe, Asia, and tropical America have also used the national park concept of conservation, so now hundreds of protected habitats exist around the world.

Marine conservation

Conservation programs for marine mammals are very important worldwide and often involve international politics. The International Whaling Commission (IWC) was established in 1946 to protect whale species from overhunting and achieve the best population levels of com-

mercial species. In this way whale hunting could carry on without all the whales being killed. However, Norway and Japan, countries that have always hunted whales, have exceeded the quotas set by the IWC many times.

▲ National park signboards provide information for visitors to St. Lucia Marine Reserve, Sodwana Bay, Natal, South Africa. Many countries practice conservation by maintaining national parks and establishing marine reserves.

TRY THIS

BACKYARD HABITAT

A basic principle of conservation programs is that more natural habitats mean more native wildlife. Large ecological reserves are often part of regional conservation plans, but you can see the positive effects by creating a habitat on a much smaller scale, such as in your backyard. To develop and maintain a backyard habitat, you need four basic things—food, water, shelter, and places for animals to have young. You also need a mixture of shrubbery, trees, and open areas to make an ecologically healthy and diverse backyard habitat that reinforces the importance of creating ecological reserves.

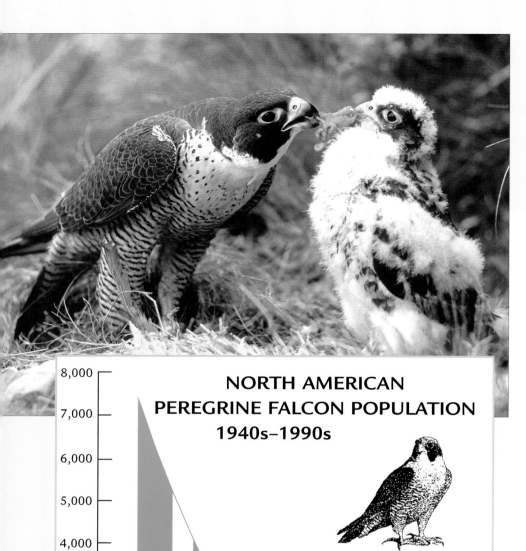

◀ *A peregrine falcon feeding its chick. In 1972 many of the pesticides that had affected the eggs of these birds were banned by the government. This action, combined with a captive-breeding program, meant their numbers steadily increased.*

NORTH AMERICAN PEREGRINE FALCON POPULATION 1940s–1990s

About 50 years ago insecticides spread through a food chain that is topped by peregrine falcons. By the 1960s peregrines were declared an endangered species. A captive-breeding program reintroduced peregrines back into the wild by 1974, when they began to breed successfully again.

Captive-breeding programs

When an animal species is threatened by extinction, conservationists may collect some of the animals and breed them in captivity. Many captive-breeding programs have been successful, including those with the peregrine falcon. In the 1950s and 1960s many farmers used pesticides to improve their crop yields, but the chemicals built up in many types of wildlife in the food web. Because they fed on contaminated prey, many birds saw their eggshells become fragile. The survival of young peregrine falcons declined, greatly reducing their numbers. In 1960 no breeding pairs were known to exist in the eastern United States. Ten years later a captive-breeding program was started using peregrines from the western United States and Europe. The program was so successful that in 1974 conservationists released the first

CAPTIVE BREEDING

Although some endangered species in zoos and other facilities have been bred successfully, then released back into the wild, some serious problems with the programs have emerged. Any excessive hunting, pollution, or habitat destruction that put the species in danger in the first place still exists in most cases. It turns out that simply adding more animals to a troubled habitat is not an effective conservation measure.

peregrine falcons back into the wild. Now peregrine falcons breed successfully in many of the places in which they once lived.

Impacts of explorers

Without conservation plans to prevent the exploitation and destruction of natural resources even small numbers of humans can wipe out species simply by moving into their native habitats and out-competing them.

Some conservation biologists think that explorers and settlers throughout the world have wiped out countless species that were easily preyed on by people. The Polynesian settlers called Maoris, for example, killed off a group of flightless bird called the moa in New Zealand. These birds were among the largest ever known, some standing more than 10 feet (3m) tall. They were not adapted to avoid human hunters; they had no

WHAT DO YOU THINK?

TURTLES AT RISK!

Marine turtles are at risk of becoming extinct. There are several causes for this, including disruption of their breeding by human interference. Some people have collected and eaten the turtle eggs they find near beaches; others have made turtle soup from adult green turtles. In Australia red foxes have preyed on turtle nests. Even though there are laws to protect the marine turtles, their population levels are still very low. In some places turtle eggs are taken indoors until they hatch, then the young turtles are released. Do you think this will solve the problem of marine turtles becoming extinct?

defenses against the settlers and could not fly away from danger. Most species of moas were extinct within 100 years of the settlers' arrival.

Panda protection

Scientists monitored the effectiveness of setting aside habitats to protect wildlife from human activities at a large ecological reserve for giant pandas in China. They found that the panda habitat had declined in quality and decreased in size since the establishment of the reserve in 1975. A rapid increase in the human population within the reserve, which led to increased tourism, removal of wood, and new road construction, was considered the main cause of the ecological degradation and habitat loss. The study reinforced the principle that effective wildlife conservation plans must always include human factors, activities, and needs.

▼ *A giant panda feeding on bamboo shoots in Sichuan Province, China. Loss of habitat is one of the main reasons for the decline in panda numbers.*

More Information

Books

Bassett, J. *Science Activities: Our Environment.* Danbury, CO: Grolier Educational, 2002.

Cefrey, H. *What If the Hole in the Ozone Layer Grows Larger?* New York: Children's Press, 2002.

Giles, B. *Parasites and Partners: Lodgers and Cleaners.* Chicago, IL: Raintree, 2003.

Martin, J. W. R. *Small Worlds: In a House.* New York: Crabtree, 2002.

Morgan, B. (ed). *Biomes Atlases.* Chicago, IL: Raintree, 2003.

Luhr, J. F. (ed). *Earth.* New York: DK Publishing, 2003.

Morgan, S. *Earth Watch: Wildlife in Danger.* New York: Franklin Watts, Inc., 2000.

Nicholson, S. *Rainforest Explorer.* Lake Mary, FL: Tangerine Press, 2001.

Pringle, L. *Global Warming: The Threat of Earth's Changing Climate.* New York: SeaStar Books, 2001.

Riley, P. *Straightforward Science: Food Chains.* New York: Franklin Watts Inc., 2003.

Websites

Edens
www.pbs.org/edens
Learn about the people, flora and fauna, and threats to some natural wonders.

Global Warming For Kids
www.epa.gov/globalwarming/ kids/index.html
Facts, games, and climate animations.

Jaguar: Lord of the Mayan Jungle
www.oneworldjourneys.com/jaguar/ index_flash.html
Join an animated expedition in the Yucatán jungle, and learn about jungle ecology and ecological preservation.

Madagascar: Biodiversity and Conservation
ridgwaydb.mobot.org/mobot/ madagascar/default.asp
Learn about why Madagascar is such a special place and ecology, evolutionary biology, and threats to biodiversity.

Monterey Bay Aquarium
www.montereybayaquarium.com
Web cams, videos, field guides, activities, games, and habitat exhibits.

NASA Earth Observatory
earthobservatory.nasa.gov/ Topics/life.html

Informative articles and spectacular satellite images show how NASA scientists are unraveling the mysteries of environmental change and many other ecological topics.

Voyage to the Deep
www.ocean.udel.edu/deepsea
Join a deep-sea expedition; with videos, photos, and multimedia tools.

Worldwide Fund for Nature
www.panda.org
Get the latest environmental news and read special features on protecting species and habitats.

Glossary

algal bloom Rapid increase in numbers of algae; can lead to poisoning of fish and other aquatic life.

bathyscaphe A spherical submersible craft used for deep-sea exploration.

biodiversity The total diversity of organisms and genes in a given area.

biomass The total weight of all the organisms in an area (or trophic level).

biome A type of major ecological community, such as a tropical rainforest, desert, or tundra.

biosphere All the parts of Earth that are able to sustain life; includes the lower atmosphere, oceans, and the surface of the land and fresh waters, and extends to a mile or so below the surface.

brackish Semisalty water, as in estuaries and deltas.

canopy Uppermost level at the tops of trees in a forest.

carbon cycle Cycle of carbon through the natural world.

carnivore An animal that eats meat.

cellulose Tough chemical that forms part of the cell walls of plants.

CFC Chemical called a chlorofluorocarbon used in the manufacture of refrigerators, polystyrene, and in aerosol spray cans; a major depleter of the ozone layer.

climate The regular weather pattern that occurs in a certain region.

community A group of different species that share a habitat.

countershading Organisms with a light top surface and a darker lower surface are said to be countershaded; common in creatures that occur in surface waters, like penguins and plankton.

dark zone Area of the deep sea to which light from the surface cannot reach.

delta Land crossed by small water channels that forms around the mouth of a river through the laying down of sediment.

ecosystem An ecological unit that comprises a community of organisms and its environment.

euphotic zone Upper layer of the ocean that receives sunlight.

filter feeder Animal that sieves fine particles from water for food.

food chain The passage of energy between organisms; a plant links to a herbivore, which in turn links to a carnivore. Energy is lost with each step.

food web A complex series of interlinked food chains.

fossil fuel Carbon-based fuel, such as oil or coal, that forms from the remains of ancient organisms.

Gaia hypothesis Idea that Earth functions as an enormous "superorganism" that maintains the conditions necessary for its survival.

greenhouse effect The rise in global temperatures caused by an increase in gases such as methane and carbon dioxide in the atmosphere.

guano A phosphorus-rich fertilizer that consists of the droppings of seabirds.

habitat The type of place in which an organism lives.

herbicide Chemical that kills off pest plants such as weeds.

herbivore Animal that feeds on plants.

hibernation To spend the winter in an inactive or dormant state.

hydrothermal vent A crack in rocks deep under the sea from which streams of very hot, chemical-laden water well up from inside the Earth's crust.

introduction The establishment of a species into a new area, sometimes through the activities of people.

mesosphere Atmospheric level between troposphere and stratosphere containing little water vapor, and where the temperature drops to -112°F (-80°C).

microhabitat A small part of a habitat that sustains a community; for example, a pool in the leaves of bromeliad plants forms a microhabitat.

migration Long-distance journey by animals such as birds, antelope, and whales either to escape harsh winter weather or to follow good sources of food.

monoculture The growing of just one crop over large areas of land.

natural selection Theory that only the organisms best suited to their environment survive to reproduce. Natural selection is the driving force behind evolution.

niche The ecological role of an organism in a community.

nitrogen fixation The incorporation by soil bacteria of nitrogen in the air into nitrate compounds that plants are able to use.

ozone layer Layer of ozone gas high in the atmosphere. It filters out harmful ultraviolet radiation from the sun.

pesticide Chemical that kills pest organisms.

photosynthesis The conversion of water and carbon dioxide into sugars in plants, using the energy of sunlight.

phytoplankton Plantlike algae that float in the surface waters of lakes or the ocean.

predator Animal that catches other animals for food.

prey Animal caught and eaten by another animal.

respiration The process of reacting food with oxygen to liberate energy; takes place inside the mitochondria of

eukaryotes or on the cell membrane of prokaryotes like bacteria.

salinity The salt content of water.

savanna A tropical grassland.

stratosphere Upper level of the atmosphere. It contains the ozone layer; extends from the mesosphere to the edge of interplanetary space.

territory Area controlled by an organism to protect food supplies or to attract a mate.

trophic level One of the links in a food chain; plants, herbivores, and carnivores are all at different trophic levels.

troposphere Lowest layer of the atmosphere. It contains most of the water vapor; clouds occur in this layer, and weather changes happen there.

tundra Cold, treeless near-polar region with a layer of permanently frozen soil just beneath the surface.

twilight zone Ocean level that receives only small amounts of light from the surface.

zooplankton Small animals that float in the surface waters of lakes or the ocean.

Set Index

Numbers in **bold** refer to volumes; page numbers in *italics* refer to picture captions.